Colombian Memoirs

OTHER BOOKS BY THE AUTHOR

Look for my next book: Colombian Memoirs: American Dreams. Other books of different stories will follow.

Colombian Memoirs

COMING TO AMERICA

PAUL A. LOPEZ

authorHOUSE

AuthorHouse™
1663 Liberty Drive
Bloomington, IN 47403
www.authorhouse.com
Phone: 1-800-839-8640

© 2012 by Paul A. Lopez. All rights reserved.

No part of this book may be reproduced, stored in a retrieval system, or transmitted by any means without the written permission of the author.

Published by AuthorHouse   07/27/2012

ISBN: 978-1-4772-5289-5 (sc)
ISBN: 978-1-4772-5352-6 (hc)
ISBN: 978-1-4772-5288-8 (e)

Library of Congress Control Number: 2012913399

Any people depicted in stock imagery provided by Thinkstock are models, and such images are being used for illustrative purposes only.
Certain stock imagery © Thinkstock.

Because of the dynamic nature of the Internet, any web addresses or links contained in this book may have changed since publication and may no longer be valid. The views expressed in this work are solely those of the author and do not necessarily reflect the views of the publisher, and the publisher hereby disclaims any responsibility for them.

DEDICATION

I DEDICATE THIS BOOK TO MY MOM AND DAD.

ACKNOWLEDGEMENTS

First I want to thank God, Jesus Christ my Savior, and the Holy Spirit our everyday companion for His constant guide through this amazing life we've had. I want to thank my wife Diana for her support and her patience with me during these five years of writing the book and typing away till the dark morning hours while she tried to sleep. Thank you my love I finally wrapped it up. I want to thank the rest of my family for helping us when we were in need, and I especially want to thank my uncle Silvio for all his help and may he Rest in Peace. Finally I want to thank my Mom and Dad for raising me and my brother in believing in God and I thank them for their courageous risks and sacrifices they made in bringing us here to the United States. I Love You Mom and Dad . . .

PREFACE

I have wanted to write this book for many years now, but it has been difficult due to certain circumstances. I always knew that my family's life has been a bit more interesting than most and that one day someone should write a book about our lives and tell our story. Who else better to tell it than one of us who lived it, and that is the reason that I decided to write this book. This book is inspired by a true story so I decided to maintain the identities of those people in this book confidential. Needless to say that the names of those mentioned are fictional and any similarities are just pure coincidence. Some of the situations and dialogue are fictional since there was no way to record them taking place. Interviewing my father took lots of time because most of our conversations took place over the phone or when I had time to visit him because he was hundreds of miles away. I finally wrote this book after four years of research and interviews. This book is about my father, a young Colombian man, his journey to the United States, the sacrifice, and the struggle in bringing his family to be with him. How a young Hispanic family had to cope with the constant fear of persecution, and threat of deportation while dealing with the pressures of poverty, and finally learning the thin line between good and bad ambition. I'd also like to warn the readers because this story does depict a life of drugs and contains some graphic material. A wise man once said, "A smart man learns from his mistakes, but a wise man learns from the mistakes of others." I hope in writing this book that those who read it will laugh, cry, make better decisions in life, and become wiser. For me it has been a long journey that has taken many years to mold me to who I am today. From the experiences lived, we know now that money comes and goes along with those supposed friends, memories are forever, family is more important, and that truly the best things in life are free. I will tell this story through my father's perspective, through his eyes, and what he remembered. I thank God for this life because it has given me the opportunity to learn a lot and to grow emotionally and spiritually. So please, I would like to invite you to sit down, relax, and take this journey with him so you can see what he saw. I am sharing our lives with the readers and hope that the readers enjoy this story. Thank you all . . .

INTRODUCTION

Colombia, South America 1955. The Golden Years, when radio was more popular than black and white TV, when food only cost cents, when cars were made from real steel, and when the Milk Man came door to door. Pereira was a small city located near the three biggest cities: Bogota, Medellin, and Cali. My father was born into a large Colombian family, a family of 14 brothers and sisters. He was the third to last child born in the family, and he was named Gilberto, a good Spanish name. Now like anywhere in the 50's people were very traditional and proper. Men in this era were very (machista) sexist, and the man was the head of the household. They were the main breadwinners with their wives at home cooking, cleaning, and taking care of the children. Families were huge in numbers back then; it was the normal size of an everyday Colombian family. After losing 2 to illness all together there were 12. Many of the older brothers and sisters were already starting families of their own when my father was born. He was brought up in a somewhat good neighborhood in a middleclass family.

My mother was also born in 1955 on a coffee farm near Pereira, on the other side of town opposite from where my father was raised. She was named Piedad, also a very Spanish name meaning Mercy. My mother was very much a merciful women always showing mercy to others, and very nurturing. She was born into a family of 12 brothers and sisters also. What can I say, my grandparents did not own a television set, and entertainment was making babies. They lost a brother when he was a young boy to an illness also making them 11. My grandparents owned a coffee farm where the older kids were raised most of their lives. They moved to Pereira when it was just being referred to as a city. At that time my mom's family was considered poor country folk, but that made them more humble people and rich at heart.

This was a time and a country where people had very little money, no technology but maybe a radio or a television set. The dirty clothes used to be washed in a big sink in the back porch, called "El Lavadero," no modern electrical technology existed yet, and only the rich could afford a car. Breakfast consisted of "Arepa con mantequilla y queso" (corn cake with butter and cheese), or

"Chocolate batido con queso y pan" (Hot chocolate with cheese, and bread) and your occasional steak and eggs. My father's family lived more comfortable than my mother's family. Because my mom's family lived in a small house with so many kids but not enough rooms or beds for all of them, it was normal for three or four brothers and sisters to sleep on the same bed. This generation of kids played with sticks, rocks, rope, rag dolls made from old shirts, and anything they could engineer from nature. They played hide and seek, ran and played outside and climbed trees, not having a care in the world. People would listen to music to pass the time, romantic slow love songs like ones by Julio Jaramillo, or Olimpo Cardenas, I remember one in particular, "Nuestro Juramento", a love song about a man promising his lady that if she dies first that he will write the story of their love with the blood of his heart. It was a very passionate time filled with passionate people. This was a tougher life back then, but more sociable. The country was mostly of the Roman Catholic religion and people's morals came from tradition, religion, and culture.

Chapter One

MY CHILDHOOD

Hello? Hello Dad? Hi it's me your son Paul. How are you? Hi son, I'm doing okay I guess. How are you, your mom, and your brother? We're all doing fine too Dad but we miss you very much. Thanks son I wish I could be with you guys too. I'm trying to be positive and have hope despite all the things that I'm facing but . . . (Sighing . . .) Yeah I know that it's not the news we wanted to hear Dad but hopefully things will get better. I hope so too son. Dad I also called you because I've been thinking a lot about what you said last time we spoke. Oh really, and what was it that I said? Dad you had mentioned something about a friend of yours that suggested to you to write a book about all this, remember? Oh yes I remember now. Well why don't you Dad? Ha ha, wow son I don't know the first thing about writing a book, or what to say. Okay then I really wanted to write it myself, and wanted to ask you what you think. Really, you want to write the book about my life son? Yes Dad but also including all of us, and how we all got here. Ha ha that's great son so when do you want to start? I've also thought about the same thing and I figured I'll interview you every chance I get and simply begin to write. Okay son so when should we start? Let's start the next time you call me that way giving me time to be better prepared ok. Ok son . . . .

Hello son it's me, how are you? Hi Dad, I'm doing well and you? Fine son, so are you ready to interview me today. Yes I am Dad I guess I'll ask you questions, and just simply answer them ok. Alright Dad can you tell me about your childhood? Tell me any funny or crazy stories you can remember too. Okay let's see. Once upon a time there was . . . No Dad (interrupting) that's not what I meant let me figure all that, all you have to do is answer my questions okay. Okay son I'm thinking and I can still remember my childhood as if it were yesterday . . . .

. . . .

Colombia 1950's. We lived in Pereira on the northeast side of town where it was considered a middleclass neighborhood, but I was born in a bad time, my family was going through economic hardship and my mother did not want to be pregnant with me. I was brought into this world in neglect from the very beginning. My father was a gambler and an odd man, and he eventually gambled all his money away. I didn't really talk to my father and I felt that my mother did not want me. He died when I was only 8 years old, and my older brothers and sisters had to help my mother with the bills. I had two younger siblings, Rosario and Juan so my mother was always busy with the babies and never had time for me. When the family would leave the house for whatever reason, they left me at home because I was too hyper. I was always getting into trouble, which earned me many beatings. Life had started tough for me from birth, but somehow I also was born with plenty of hope and a great sense of humor for life. I always made jokes about my unfortunate situations and how I would make it big one day and win the praises of my family.

    I began going to school and I used to walk an hour away, like 10 blocks, or it was probably more, up and down hill, in the rain, sleet and hail, if it snowed in Colombia I would've walked in the snow too. There were no school buses, and money for the city bus was out of the question. I had no money for new shoes and all that walking wore holes on the bottom of my shoes. I had to improvise with what I had and I would cut cardboard out and put it inside to stop my foot from touching the ground, you know, to avoid ripping my socks, if I had socks on that day that is, ha ha ha (internal laughing). When I went to school I didn't have money for lunch, and my friends would sometimes give me something of theirs, but most of the time I had to hold my hunger until I got home. Most days I remember that when I was hungry, I would drink lots of water to trick my stomach into feeling full, a habit that often would get me sick with parasites in my stomach eventually causing ulcers. After school I would get home with such an appetite that I would go into the kitchen looking for anything that got in my way so I could devour it. Milk in these times was delivered by the Milkman in those glass jugs; you know which ones I'm talking about. It was a luxury to have milk and it was only served at breakfast by the drops, maybe in your coffee or in your "Agua de Panela con Leche" (sugarcane water with milk). In Colombia "Agua Panela" is a very traditional beverage that has nourished just about every happy soul that had the privilege of being born here; it is the Colombian version of tea. Back to the milk story; one afternoon here I was, 10 years old nearly starving, my reasoning not working correctly, and my survival instinct possessing me I desperately searched for food. On top of the fridge I find where my mother saved some milk left from the mornings so she could have later for her and my baby brother Juan. My hunger painted a picture in my mind of me chugging the pitcher of warm milk until it was dry, but then my conscience woke me up and then I had a different picture of my mother taking a belt to my behind. What do I do? I would carefully weigh my options in my evil little brain, what if this, what if that? My inner little voice would say "Don't do it!" and I thought about taking a beating. "No! I can't drink my baby brother's milk, he needs it, but so do I!" My hunger yelled with disapproval. As I was about to walk away I had an epiphany. I know what to do! I will drink some milk and fill the rest with water so that way no one will ever find out. I ignored my inner little voice and that day I drank a little milk and poured some water in it and the milk mixed in with it great . . . Heeuuu . . . That was close, nobody will notice. So every afternoon that I would get home hungry I had me some warm milk. I would drink some and mix in some water. I did this for quite a while hoping that I would never get caught, until one day I was enjoying the delicious pitcher of milk too much, there I was chugging away with milk dripping from the sides of my mouth, I accidently drank too much. "Oh no!" I said to myself, "what am I going to do now?" I mixed in the water but it looked kind of watery, there was no way I could get any milk so I kept my fingers crossed and left it. I was so scared that my mother would notice, but I had no other choice, I left the watery milk where I found it and hoped for the best. My nerves were driving me crazy all day. Later that afternoon my mother walked in the kitchen to drink the milk, so she got it from off the top of the refrigerator where she thought it was safe. I was nervous as she poured a glass. I was sweating by then so I had to leave. As I was walking away, I hear my mother say, "For the love of God! Every day this milk tastes more and more like water." She had not noticed what I had done! I thought to myself how lucky I was as I laughed and ran into the street.

    1960's, Pereira was built over several steep mountains and the streets were also awkwardly steep. The houses were built connected to each other side by side to conserve space, mountains surrounded the city, and there was no space for kids to play. That didn't stop us from playing Futbol, (soccer) in the street, dodging cars, and sometimes breaking neighbor's windows with the ball. It was an adventurous childhood; for example when the soccer ball would get away from us, it would roll forever down the steep hills faster than we ever could run, and disappear in the distance claimed by the other neighborhood kids. Sometimes we would have a soccer ball roll into our street from the neighborhood kids from up the hill, and that's what we played with until it would roll away. We would ride bikes or roller skate down the steep hills hoping not to fall and get erased by the gravel or get hit by any cars as we flew by the intersections. We also went to rivers to swim, jump and dive from high cliffs or trees or any high place. The rivers were very dangerous and we had to be careful not to get taken by the strong currents or whirlpools and disappearing into the curvy snake rivers. There was one time when we were swimming at a river, I was in the water over my head and I usually would use the rocks on the bottom to push off of and out so I could get to the surface. This day I tried doing that and I felt a soft surface that was being taken by the current in the deep, I felt it with my feet and wondered what it was, so I dove under to feel what it was. When I grabbed it, it was large, but when I felt the unmistakable feeling of clothes I knew right away it was a person. I was immediately scared and sick to my stomach. It was a dead body and it eventually floated to a shallow part in the river, but me and my friends didn't know if it was somebody that drowned, or a dead body that was thrown into the river to float away. We didn't want to find out either, so we left quickly that day. This is the country I was born in, where life was more exciting but fragile and death was a normal thing. Life threatening situations happened all the time, and it was normal. Unforgettable moments like one that happened in my neighborhood, a night that two neighbors got into an argument and it turned into a machete fight! Yes, I said "machete fight." I still can remember the sparks on the street from when they would strike the pavement with their machetes. It was like an action scene from a movie, two fighters with swords slashing at each other. The fight ended ugly with them having to rush to the hospital and if I can remember correctly I think one man did die, and that family moved out from the neighborhood soon after. This was Colombia in the 1960's so it was common for that sort of thing; I guess it was because the gun was not that accessible yet, it was sad but true.

 My family was Catholic; you would never see a Catholic home missing the Crucifixion, a picture of The Sacred Heart of Jesus, a candle of the Virgin Mary, and of the other Saints. I remember going to church on Sundays, and observing the sacraments, like Baptisms, and the First Communion and things like that. It gave me something good to believe in and it also gave me great memories from the ceremonies and the celebrations that our families had afterwards. We were fortunate enough to own a TV back then, the picture was in black and white but it didn't matter, it was an awesome invention. I was raised watching American movies, movies with Paul Newman, like the Towering Inferno, also John Wayne, and Steve McQueen. I thought they were great; I especially liked Steve McQueen movies, The Great Escape, Papillion, etc . . . I remember watching American movies and seeing how nice the houses were and the wide streets with no pot holes, the huge cities with their tall skyscrapers and I fell in love with USA. We called it "La USA" or "Nueva York", even though the states were many, most people could only remember New York. I told myself that one day when I was older that I would have to live there if I wanted to have a nice life, maybe even be in movies. This was my dream, to leave Colombia and become an actor in the United States of America, because life here was very hard, and I didn't see myself living in Colombia with a family. In the streets I would see the ugliness of the world. The beggars, the sick and maim in the streets with their obvious diseases showing for all to see, their missing limbs where they had been amputated, or the maimed thieves, survivors of violent retaliation from their victims that left them worse off. Like the one guy who had a sink hole wound under his nose above his mouth where his lip and nose would nearly touch, or the guy walking around with a colostomy bag because he had been shot for stealing, and the bullets ruined his colon. There were homeless people even homeless children living in the streets hustling, using drugs to keep themselves warm and to numb the pain of hunger, and struggling to put food in their mouths. I saw the disgust in the people's faces and the neglect the world gave them. That people with money who were successful were called Ladies and Gentlemen, but the poor were looked down upon and were treated less than the others like stray dogs. I was old enough to know what made this world go round, and that was MONEY and I wanted lots of it, because I didn't want to be treated like a stray dog. I was at least 10 years old when I started to work during my school vacations. There were no child labor laws so I worked however long I wanted to. I first had a job selling women's purses in the streets, then I worked in a bakery and I did it so I could buy myself things. I didn't need to ask my mother or brothers and sisters for too much, so it kept me more independent. Now that I was making some cash on my own I wanted to travel a bit and thought I would go visit my sister Lia in Cali just to see how other cities were. Cali is about 3 hours away from Pereira in a bus and my sister picked me up at the station. My sister was married and her husband had a good business which in return gave them money so they lived really nice. My sister's house was amazing and they even had a maid that helped with the daily chores. I was not there for more than an hour when I noticed that her husband had a very nice 10speed road bike. My eyes quickly set on this man's bike and I had an amazing vision of me riding the grease out of it until receiving butt blisters. Colombia has produced some of the world's best cyclists due to our amazing Andes Mountains and these dedicated individuals riding their road bikes until the blisters on their butts bled. I too aspired to be one of those amazing athletes and developing butt blisters from my tenacious dedication. So I asked him if I could ride his bike, but he said no because he had sold it and was holding it until the buyer had all the money. So of course I did what any smart kid what've done; I waited for him to leave. When he left the house it gave me the nerve to ask my sister, but she also said no. "Ok, I tried" I said to myself. But wait he's going to sell it, meaning I won't be able to ride it ever! I thought if I ride it and bring it back quickly nobody will ever find out. Again I didn't listen to my inner little voice telling me not to do it, maybe because I was disrespecting this man's property, not to mention his authority, but I said whatever man I'll be right back, what could ever go wrong. I snuck the bike out of the house and I began riding this nice 10speed down the street, up and down the block. It was shiny cherry red, with white hand grips, and white lettering. It read "Peugeot" on the frame, what a strange name for a bike, it sounded French or something I guess. This French bike was amazing, so smooth, and quick, the gears were nice looking, and the pedals hugged my feet nice and firm. It was incredible how this bike felt and became like a part of me. I was focusing on the bike and rode several blocks away not noticing that I rode past my safe zone. I forgot that I was in a different city and no one knew who I was. I was only focusing on how awesome I looked on that bike. Well I imagine that the local thief thought he could look real awesome on the bike too. He didn't hesitate to run up to me, push me to the ground, and snatch my sorry little butt off that nice 10speed. He punched me in the stomach when I tried defending myself and as I lay in the street trying to catch my breath he rode off into a cloud of dust never to be seen again. OH NO!!! What just happened! I was just robbed and punched in the stomach. I thought to myself as I gasped for air, "THIEF!" I yelled, although it was too late and nobody would have helped me anyway because I was not from around there. A scary thought popped into my head "I'd better get home before someone else tries to steel my shoes or something worse!" I got to my sister's house and the fear that was running through my head was unbelievable. I took this man's bike and now it was stolen. My sister answered the door and quickly asked, "Where's the bike!" I couldn't hold it and I cried, "I was robbed!" My sister was so mad and yelled at me as she yanked me inside from my hair. Her husband was even madder when he heard what happened. That man turned RED and he started yelling at me, and called me all sorts of things except a child of God. He said something like: "YOU

EVIL LITTLE DEMON! YOU GOT MY PEUGEOT STOLEN AFTER I HAD SOLD IT TO SOMEONE! I'M GONNA DESTROY YOU!!!" How was I supposed to know that it was so expensive that it was a famous Peugeot? He kicked me out of the house at that moment; I think it was to avoid killing me. If he did want to hurt me then I preferred leaving than getting my butt kicked again. Now the problem I had was how was I, a 10 year old, going to get home? I walked forever until I reached the bus terminal and took a bus back to Pereira. In the bus I was hoping that the news of the stolen bike would not get home. But I decided that I should at least enjoy this 3 hour bus ride before I would get home to the nightmare of my reality; that I had gotten that man's extremely expensive French bike stolen. Finally I got back home where the scary reality awaited me. My family had heard the bad news and my older brother Joel was waiting for me with the belt in his hands. I finally did earn those butt blisters I wanted but not from riding the bike. Boy was I ever sorry I took that bike, he was a Colombian Marine and he had all those muscles that go along with being a Marine, those same muscles and the belt left my behind hurting for days. After that, I decided that I didn't want to travel anywhere anymore just to avoid problems, especially beatings from my brother Joel, the Colombian Marine, and the belt. The "BELT" was this simple long, smooth, thick, black leather clothing accessory used to keep your pants up that in hands of enraged parents would become your worst nightmare. Its ability to whip at you with its flexibility leaving you defenseless against its wrath and still so devastating to the skin was mind-blowing. Its bonus too was that it still caused pain through several pairs of jeans. It was almost worth adding that sales pitch to the "Belt" telling the consumer that it served several purposes like steering your kids straight. As for my older brother he was a strict regimented man with a tough voice that when he spoke he demanded respect, but from me he got fear. Now that I think about it, my whole family was strict and regimented and they all spoke with tough voices and they all demanded respect. I guess my mother had to be tough with us since she was left a widow with so many kids. I grew older and I became more responsible, I wanted to make a name for myself so my family could feel proud of me by moving to the United States and making lots of money. My older brother Silvio took care of my brother Juan and I and he taught us how to take care of ourselves. He told us to stick together, and that blood was thicker than water, that family was forever and friends just came and went. So no matter our differences, we had to always forgive each other and look out for one another; so we did. He said these things because we had two of our family members die while we were still young. Our older brother Fulbio died of an illness when he was a young boy, and my older sister Sulma committed suicide because of a broken heart. She actually swallowed a bunch of matches, those you can light by striking any rough surface. She got really sick from swallowing the matches so she took some laxative to get rid of them quicker, but unfortunately she died. The Doctor said that the mix of the matches with the laxative was the reason that she died. My brother Silvio wanted us to watch out for one another to keep these things from happening again.

Colombia was an economically poor country but it was very rich in various types of exports. Colombia is still famous for its gold and its beautiful emeralds, also Colombia is rich with fruits, vegetables, coffee, orchids, and with other plants that since then have become illegal to grow. There was the Marihuana plant, the Poppy plant, which produces Heroine, and the famous Coca plant, which produces Cocaine. The Coca and the Poppy plant were nice plants because they had nice flowers. The Coca grew just about everywhere and it was planted in the median of two of Pereira's main streets. Soon after the news broke, stating that they were being used to make powerful drugs the plants were all removed and destroyed the very next day. The Era of the Colombian Drug Lord had begun. You would hear on the news, that certain people were exploiting the illegal crops and making money, but I was just a kid and that stuff never interested me.

It was the 1970's; music, cigarettes, and alcohol were a social must. I was a teenager and dancing was how we partied, you heard Colombian Cumbia and Salsa in every neighborhood, party, and club. I remember listening to songs like "El Canoero" and "El Pescador de Baru" by Los Warahuaco, "Boquita de Caramelo," "Tabaco y Ron," and "Colegiala" by Rodolfo y los Hispanos, "Caballo Viejo" by Roberto Torres, and "El Preso" by Fruco y sus Tesos" and "Sobre las Olas" by The Latin Brothers. So many great Colombian music artists and other Latin American artists like Hector Lavo, Willy Colon, Oscar de Leon, Celia Cruz, and El Gran Combo were heard . . . All these great Latin American groups ruled the night and man did we love to party. I would hear this music on the weekends coming from peoples' houses in the neighborhoods and these parties would last till sun rise!

My sister Rosario was working in a paper factory and some of her coworkers would get together to party on the weekends, and Piedad was one of her friends. I remember when I met Piedad; she was this beautiful young, timid girl, with straight jet black hair and honey colored eyes. She was also a great dancer and that's how I got to meet her. I was a big flirt so I tried really hard to get her attention, but I was more annoying than anything because she wouldn't even give me the time of day. That didn't stop me from trying, I was persistent and I knew I wanted her to be my girlfriend. When the weekend would come around I would ask my sister Rosario, "So where's the party tonight?" The only reason I asked was to know if Piedad would be going too. My interest was set on this beautiful Colombian girl and trying to win her heart was priority number one. Eventually I met all of Piedad's family. We became a group of friends that would hang out and go to trips and parties together. After a year of me trying to win Piedad's heart, she finally warmed up to me and she became my girlfriend. We were growing up together and going through high school at the time. The years went by quickly and I was graduating from high school already. I got a job working as an accountant assistant for a small business while I tried to attend college, but my relationship with Piedad got serious. We were in love and I asked her to marry me, and she said yes. We had a small wedding and soon we moved in together in a small house that we rented. The real world was tough, Piedad worked and I worked and took some courses to see if one day I would graduate from College. Unfortunately we didn't see much progress for a future in Colombia because times were tough and we had a disadvantage, we were dirt poor. We did not have much help from our families either since they had families of their own to care for. Now more than ever I wanted desperately to leave Colombia and move to the United States. All I knew was that I wanted to move to AKA: "La USA" and AKA: "Nueva York," no matter how or what I had to do, I had to do it for my family to give my children better opportunities in life.

Chapter Two

CROSSING THE BORDER

Hello Paul, it's me again. Hi Dad, how are you? I heard the great news, how do you feel? I'm better now that I'm out but I'm still far from you guys though. I know but just wait and see things will get better I hope. Ok so where were we son? Yes you were telling me about when you crossed through El Hueco. Ok yes how could I forget that adventurous moment . . . .

. . . .

Colombia 1975, I was 20 years old and I was married to Piedad. We were living pay check to pay check, moving from place to place, and we were hoping that things would get better. Piedad also believed in God and being brought up in the Catholic Church we knew that when things were out of your hands you should ask God for help. We prayed for a miracle, for things to change for the better because we were feeling the pressures of poverty and of having no real future. I began asking around town on how I could get to "La USA" (The USA), AKA: "Nueva York" (New York), or "El Otro Lado" (The Other side), and you could only get there through "El Hueco" (The Hole). Till this day in Colombia this is a common question like asking how to get to Downtown, but the correct question was not "how to get to the U.S.?" it was "how much was it going to cost?" The price in these days was around $2,000 dollars per person. I was crushed, when was I ever going to save that much money for Piedad and me to get to the States? My hope was getting weaker and weaker as the months went by but finally, Silvio, my older brother called me one day unexpectedly and he sounded very excited on the phone. He was trying to tell me something, "Gilberto I got a travel visa! I am going to La USA!" "What", I asked . . . I couldn't believe his words. "Did you say that you're going to the United States?" I had to make sure that I heard him correctly. He said it again louder, "Yes Guevon I am leaving to the United States!" I felt this huge relief, like a ton of bricks had been lifted off my back. I knew that with Silvio on the other side that it would make things a little easier for us to get there one day. So those in the family that had enough money filled an application with the U.S. Embassy for a travel visa. Amazingly Piedad's sister, Maria had also been given a visa to go to the United States. This was all great news for all of us but it still didn't help us that much. We were still in Colombia and needed things to change fast. My question now was, "how was I going to get Piedad and me to La USA?" The time came when both my brother Silvio and Piedad's sister Maria left for the States. My brother headed to Connecticut and my sister-in-law headed to New Jersey. They eventually got jobs and began to send money to help with the bills.

Christmas came and went and the New Year 1976 was knocking at our door. Piedad and I were turning 21 and the news of a baby on the way was also knocking at our door. That was such great news for us because we were going to be parents! We wondered if it was going to be a boy or a girl, and we began looking for names. I had the hope that we would be raising our children in the U.S. so I wanted to give our children American names. I did not like my name at all, Gilberto, that was an ugly name, but few of us like our names anyway. I didn't want my children to have those long Hispanic names either, you know, your child having to say "My name is Fernando Roberto Eduardo Dominguez, but everybody calls me FRED for short". I didn't want my children to be called "Alphabet" either. "Hey Alphabet come over here." or "Hey Alphabet, pass me the ketchup." So we looked for common American names. Piedad used to watch American movies with me and she thought that Paul Newman was handsome, so she wanted her boy's name to be Paul, she said, "but to give it a Colombian twist he'll have the middle name of Andres". Paul Andres sounded nice, a little American with some flavor. I even wanted to change my name to Bryan, but Piedad would laugh at me and say "Okay Bryan with that Hispanic nose you have." which I was very sensitive about. My nose was a little bigger than required to breathe and I wanted to get rid of that too. Piedad was pregnant and now more than ever I felt the need to provide for my family. I would pray at night that God would bless us and give me the opportunity to be a good provider for my family.

Silvio called me up from "La USA" one night to talk. "So Silvio how are you doing up there?" "Yeah, I'm ok but I miss the family a lot, you know." So I asked the question, "I wanted to ask you if you could lend me the money to come through "El Hueco" (The Hole) through the Mexican border?" He said, "If you're willing to get through that, I'll try to send you the money." I didn't hesitate and said "Of course I am willing!" "Gilberto but you're gonna have to give me the time to save up that much money, and I don't know how long it will take me." "That's fine, I'll wait, thanks brother." Now I just had to wait for the money. Nine months went by and Paul was born. That was a happy time for Piedad and I, and our family was very supportive. We could not afford our apartment anymore, so we stopped paying the rent and waited to get kicked out. It didn't take very long to get the boot from the landlord. But thankfully, God gave us a lending hand and Piedad's parents told us to move in with them. Thank God they had an extra room in their house since most of their children were grown and had moved out. Being a father was great, but I was upset with myself for not being able to take care of my family the way I wanted to care for them. Every night before I went to bed I would say a prayer for that money to get to me. Every day when I got home from work I would check if I had a letter from Silvio, but nothing. Finally one day Silvio called me, "Hey little brother, how are you?" "I'm doing fine, just trying to get by you know how it is over here." Ok Gilberto, I got the money for you, and I'll be wiring it to you this week, ok." "Thanks Silvio! When I get there, I'll repay every penny, ok, I promise." Silvio added, "Don't worry about that right now just focus on getting here and be very careful out there, alright." I said, "A la mano de Dios!" (In God's hands!) We were happy about the news, but Piedad was very nervous because she was going to have to care for my son Paul by herself while I tried to bring them to me. Piedad said to me, "Promise that you won't forget about me and the baby, think of us when you're lonely and know that we love you. Without you, we will be lost in this cruel world." I knew she was right and promised that I would keep them in my heart and would sacrifice my all to get them by my side.

Once the money arrived, I knew what I had to do. I made the arrangements over the phone with the Coyotes, that's the name of the human traffickers, and I had to take a plane to Mexico City; I was on my way to get through "El Hueco". It was all so surreal to me; I couldn't believe what was going on, and that I was really making plans to get to "Nueva York." I had my plane ticket to Mexico City and the rest was pure mystery. I felt my stomach turn with anxiety not knowing what could happen. Maybe robbed in Mexico, be put in jail, it could all be a hoax to steal people's money, possibly get lost in the desert and die. These were some of the risks that I was facing. I have a saying, "you can't live life if you don't risk a little." Well I knew that this was a very big risk and that we were going to be able to live life for real after all this was over! I hoped that this was the case for us anyway. Piedad and I talked a lot and we had a little plan, I would work real hard to bring them with me. The week before leaving I was saying my goodbyes to the family and trying not to be so nervous for the trip. The time came, I was at the airport waiting to leave for Mexico City, and all the family was there saying their goodbyes and wishing me good luck. Piedad hugged me and gave me a big kiss and told me to remember my promise that I would not forget about her and the baby. I told her I remembered and we cried as the flight attendant asked for passengers to board the airplane. I was nervous and scared because I was leaving my wife and baby behind to a future that was uncertain. Would I be caught in Mexico, at the border, in the U.S.? Would I be able to find work, save money, get a place for all of us, and be able to bring them with me? Or would I die in the desert or be killed by thieves. I didn't know the answer to any of these questions. All I had was hope, will, and a positive mind that my future was in God's hands. I told Piedad "I Love You" and walked out on the runway to the airplane. My family waved goodbye to me from the airport balcony, as I walked to the plane. My eyes watered but I held in the tears, being hopeful that I soon would be on U.S. soil. The plane backed out on the runway and we began making our way down to one side. The plane turned around and started speeding up to get enough take off speed. The plane took off and we were in the air. I could see the city shrinking in the distance, and the streets with its traffic getting smaller and smaller. The sky looked beautiful with the great green mountains in the distance surrounding Pereira, and the clouds touching the tops of the mountains making it hard to see the snow on top of the nearby volcano "El Nevado del Ruiz." Colombia was a beautiful country, but I needed work and a better future.

We made a stop in Bogota, the Capital of Colombia. All international flights made a stop there to go through customs and get your passport stamped. There I saw customs where they ask you all sorts of questions. The customs agent asked me, "So what are your plans in Mexico?", and I told the guy, "I am going on a trip to visit the city and maybe go see some of the Aztec ruins". "Okay, have a nice time", he said. I thought to myself "that was easy." I boarded the plane again and we took off for Mexico. "Wow, here I go", I said, "now I could try some of that Mexican food which I hear is delicious." I slept in the flight because it was going to be a while. We flew over Central America but when the clouds weren't blocking the view all I could see was green mountains. Hours went by and the Pilot came over the intercom and said that we were beginning our descent into Mexico City. My heart began thumping against my chest; I said a little prayer and hoped for the best. Mexico City was visible from the plane now, and it was a huge city. Evening was approaching but you could still see the city surrounded by the mountains like in Colombia. We landed and the plane came into the docking station where the plane finally settled. The Pilot said, "Welcome to Mexico City Federal District", blah, blah, blah . . . I didn't hear the rest because I was busy thinking about what I had to do next. The International Airport was real nice, I went to baggage claim, got my one bag and made my way to the line for the customs agents. "What is your business in Mexico City?" he asked, and I replied, "I am visiting the country, and going site seeing." "How long are you staying?" he asked again, "I am staying a few weeks", I answered. The customs agent looked at me suspiciously and asked why I was alone, but I told him that I was single and wanted to have fun in Mexico. He let me go, so I took my baggage, got a taxi and left the airport. The next step was going to a certain hotel and calling the contact in Mexico City. I arrived at the hotel and got my room, and in the room I quickly called the contact. This man on the other line sounded calm so it made me feel calm. I guess it was because he did this so often that he had no need to worry. He told me to get some food and to be back at a certain time, and that he would call me later. I said, "Okay time to go try that famous Mexican food I heard so much about." I went out in the city and took in the sites near the hotel, got some food and it was very good. You had to be careful not to get anything too spicy because your lips would melt off and your intestines would pay later. I made that mistake that day, but I was young and my lips adapted quickly, but my intestines reminded me later not to make that mistake again. Mexico City was big and a very nice city, with all the old Spanish architecture and new buildings that filled the night's sky. The time went quickly and I had to return to the hotel. When I got back I waited for the contacts call again. This calm man called me again and told me my next move. I had to stay there the night and in the morning he would come to pick me up. Well with that said I then thought, "Hey I'm not letting a night in Mexico City go to complete waste." I went down to the lobby where there was a lounge playing some old Mexican Rancheras, I went to the bar and had me some beers. Maybe not a very good idea since I would probably not eat or drink water for days and alcohol would only dehydrate me. When I looked around the lounge, I saw a familiar face from Pereira. It was actually a co-worker of mine that I had worked with a few years ago. "Hey Dario what are you doing here?" "Gilberto what in the world, I can't believe that you're here too." He was with his sister, Claudia, and they were heading for the border to get into the States also. We started talking about the trip, well what else were we going to call it, the migration, the infiltration; there was no nice name for this so we called it a trip. "We really hope this is for real and that it's not some scam", he said, and I thought the same thing. There was a young couple also in the bar. "Those others are going too but they're not from Colombia," Dario told me. We met the other people and I began drinking with them and having normal conversation. The young couple was from Mexico. We talked for a few hours but then we called it a night. "Goodnight Gilberto," "Goodnight Dario, and be careful who you talk to. I'll see you guys in the morning," I said. We all said goodnight and went to our rooms.

The morning came and I went to the lobby for the complimentary breakfast. Eggs Rancheros, some type of breakfast burritos, coffee, fruit, and fruit juices were on the menu. Delicious, I love to eat and I quickly dug in. "Good morning Gilberto", the others were there also eating breakfast, "hey good morning guys." We all sat together and ate and when we were all done we waited for the Coyote to pick us up. It was around 7:00 in the morning when the Coyote came for us. He told us to get rid of our luggage and only take a small back pack with one change of clothes. That made sense, so I picked something simple and got rid of the rest. It was hard to let go of my clothes since it took me a while to buy them. We all got into the truck that the coyote came in and we drove for hours, going north to our destination, the Mexican/American border. We arrived at some small city called Piedras Negras that was south of the border. This city was surrounded by desert, but not those sandy deserts. It was more like the rugged, tough terrain, rocky, with occasional trees, and lots of cactuses and of course the mountains in the distance. The Coyote took us to a farm, or hacienda in Spanish, that he and his entourage owned near the city. We rested there the night, ate, and drank lots of water for the trip ahead.

In the morning the roosters crowed and the Coyote came to wake us up and told us to shower but to wear the same clothes as yesterday because we were going to get dirty today. We had no idea what was ahead of us. We had to leave the truck at the hacienda and we walked to the city. The Coyote told us that we had to hide from the Mexican Police looking for people in groups heading for the border. "Alright where do we hide?" Dario asked, and the Coyote said, "We are going to have to go through the sewers so we can make it closer to the border without getting caught." We all thought the same thing, "The sewers!" but we were all willing to get across no matter how we did it. "Okay we'll follow you sir," we said. The Coyote lead us to a specific street and when there was nobody looking, he opened the sewer manhole cover and told us to get in quick. We did what he said hoping and trusting that he was not going to abandon us later. We got inside and it was a small sewer, dark, wet, and it stunk like Mexican intestine aftermath, you know, like what a sewer would smell like. The Coyote had a flash light and we quickly realized that the tunnels were very small and that we were going to have to crawl. "I hope this is just a bad joke." one of the ladies said. Unfortunately it was not a joke, it was a nightmare. That was the most disgusting thing I had ever done. The Coyote began leading us through the small tunnels on his hands and knees, so we got on our hands and knees in the sewer water. It was very difficult when I felt the water touch my knees, and then my hands were in the water too. I had to keep myself from vomiting although some others did. The women began crying because it was so dirty and wet. We started making our way through the dark tunnels of this sewer underneath Piedras Negras towards the border. Here we were on our hands and knees in sewer water, it smelled bad, it was dark, the roaches were pretty big, "La Cucaracha." I hate roaches now more than ever. The rats were even bigger, but at least they had the common sense to run away from us, unlike the roaches which would crawl over our hands and our legs. "Aaahhhh!!!" the women would scream on occasion, and the Coyote finally yelled at them, "Hey!" then he whispered, "stop screaming damn it, before you get us caught!" They cried some more and we comforted them by telling them, "we're almost there ladies, not much longer." I was glad that I was alone on this trip, because I couldn't imagine Piedad and my son having to suffer like this. We were in this sewer crawling for about two hours now, we had gotten used to the smell by now when the Coyote told us that we were almost there. We were relieved to hear that because all of us had vomited at least once and that was not good. We came up to the main sewer exit where we finally climbed out of. It was still in the afternoon when we got out and we were out of the city somewhere in the forest/desert. I stretched; glad to be out of that sewer and all I wanted now was to get clean. I know that the others had the same in mind. We continued moving and we stopped at a small stream where we rested. The women wanted to change but the Coyote said, "Not yet, we still have a lot to go." The women argued that they had just gotten out of a sewer. "You paid me to get you over the border safe and sound, did you not!" he said and the women replied, "yes, but," "No buts, you better trust me or you will be left for dead because I am not going to stop for sick people!" The guys added, "He is right, we better listen to him because he has experience," "Okay" the women agreed. We got clean as much as we could in the little stream and we kept moving. It was hot during the day so we tried to stay in the shade from the trees. We walked through the forest for hours, but I had no idea how this Coyote guided us through the forest because it all looked the same to us. "Hey look, pineapples!" One of the guys saw that there were some pineapples growing in a field. Without hesitation, we took to those pineapples like poor starving people, and pulled some out of the ground. That was the easy part, but we didn't have a knife. Before this day I had taken knives for granted and never had appreciated them as much as I did that moment. How do you get inside a pineapple without hurting yourself, it was almost comical. Seeing Dario trying to bite his way through was hilarious, but its peel proved to be tougher than human teeth. We struggled with those pineapples for minutes until the Coyote said, "hey guys do you wanna use my knife?" "What, how come you didn't say anything?" Claudia asked. The Coyote laughed and simply said, "You never asked me." Claudia was mad at the guy, but I thought it was pretty funny. Man we were hungry, so we tore into those pineapples and they were delicious. We ate quite a few of them and we enjoyed them. Have you ever heard of Murphy's Law? It says that in a situation if something can go wrong, then it will go wrong. Well Murphy had tagged along with us that day. Our intention in eating those pineapples was to hydrate a little and the flavor was a bonus, but what we didn't know is that those pineapples gave us some serious diarrhea. Now we had to make all these emergency pit stops in the forest. Thank God it was a forest, and not a desert where there's no shade or privacy. Of course we didn't have toilet paper; we had to use the leaves, the foliage, whatever was in reach. Losing too much water was dangerous in this situation, so we were pretty concerned. Fortunately for us the Coyote had some water saved from the stream earlier that day. He was nice enough to keep us hydrated and to keep us going. We had been walking for hours and we finally reached the Rio Grande. Wow, I thought, I am really here at the Rio Grande. The Coyote told us, "Now we must hurry because police patrol the river." We ran to the river to get across it quickly, but the river was not little, it was actually pretty wide. The Coyote ran to a big bush and some trees and he pulled on a rope that ran from a tree under the water to the other side to another tree. We had to grab the rope and pull ourselves across and keep the current from taking us away. So we had to cross the river a few at a time. We all crossed and it took us only a few minutes to get across the river, and here I thought that was going to be the hardest part, but in reality it was really simple. He put the rope away and hid it with branches and loose leaves, and we were walking again. It was getting dark now and the Coyote told us that we were almost at the place we were going to rest the night. That was good to hear but when he told us that once we had crossed the river we were on US soil, that was the best feeling I had in a long time. We were in Eagles Pass, Texas in the United States of America. We all cried a little out of happiness because we had made it across, but we knew that we were not finished yet. When were we going to finish this long and painful hike in the forest? We all asked ourselves that question because we were so exhausted. My feet hurt and I could feel the blisters popping and the liquid running through my toes. I wanted to be at my brother's already in Connecticut and not out here in the forest with strangers and a Mexican human trafficker. Night approached and it was cold out here in the forest/desert, and I heard a coyote howling at the moon. Not our Coyote, the human trafficker, but the real thing. For that brief moment I looked around in the night and what I could see in the darkness was the moon, which was a crescent moon not giving too much of her light, and the stars flashing down at us. Other than that all I could see was the silhouette of the mountains and everything else was black. The women were scared about the coyotes and began asking about all the other animals in the desert, like tarantulas, scorpions, snakes, and of course the mountain lions. The others bugged me a little, but coyotes and mountain lions really scared the crap out of me. We walked a lot closer to one another and we were very alert. The Coyote started making his way to some bushes like he knew where he was going in the pitch black. We had no idea how this man could guide us through the night and know where he was going and how to find things that they left hiding for crossing the border. We followed him to some dark brush and he disappeared inside of it. "Where did he go?" Claudia asked. Then his voice came from the bushes, "come inside now." So I followed his voice and noticed that we were walking into a small cave. Man if I thought it was dark outside, it was really dark inside of this cave. All of us walked inside of the cave but we had to lower our heads because the inside was only some 4 feet high. The Coyote told us, "You will be resting here the night and I will pick you up tomorrow." That worried us and we all thought that this guy was going to abandon us out here and leave us for dead. "When will you be back," Dario asked. The Coyote responded, "When it is safe to come and get you." The Coyote told us not to leave the cave because border patrol would be patrolling the area. He also said not to wander off, because when he would come back he was not going to wait for any one. He gave us a code word, that when we would hear the word "Cinco" meaning five, because there were five of us; that we could come out of the cave. He left us in the cave with no light and little water, but we were so tired that we just went to sleep. As I was sleeping I was woken up by pain, "Ouch! Aahh! What is that?" We were all yelling about the same thing, we were getting bitten or stung by something,

"Ants!" We were covered in ants and they were biting hard. I was jumping up and down and shaking the ants off. I couldn't see the others but I imagine they were doing the same, because that's what it sounded like. We were all grunting and cursing while we shook off the ants. So we moved from that spot hoping there were no more ants and went back to sleep.

The next day the sun's rays entered the cave and woke us up. Now that it was day, we could see the ant pile that we had been lying in. The cave was small and narrow, but we couldn't leave the cave not even to pee. The cave got smaller and darker towards the end, so we decided to designate the back of the cave as the restroom. We waited patiently for the Coyote, but after hours of waiting we were getting nervous. We were starving and our water had finished, and the cave was beginning to smell like our urine. We were in the wilderness with no food or water; these were the ingredients for death. I think I began praying for that man to come back for us and get us to safety. We had been waiting all day, it was probably around 4pm and we were really scared, the women began crying thinking that we had been abandoned. Suddenly we all heard someone yelling, "Cinco!" "Did you hear that?" we all asked ourselves. We yelled back, "Cinco!" "Cinco," we heard it again so we all ran out of the cave. I couldn't believe my eyes. We were near a highway inside Texas already, and we had no idea. The Coyote was yelling at us from a truck on the highway, signaling us to run to the truck quickly to avoid getting caught. We ran to that truck with all the strength that was left in our starving, thirsty, dirty, stinky, blistered, and ant bitten bodies. We climbed in the back of the truck and ducked inside, all of us had made it. We did not lose anybody, get robbed, nor get caught. I thanked God for getting us across safely. Inside the flatbed of that pickup truck, we all laid down face up; we laughed, cried, hugged one another and we were thankful to be alive and conquering "El Hueco". We were all so very happy to be in the United States.

I had a dream of the Statue of Liberty receiving all immigrants and giving us the chance to a life of liberty, without oppression, and without so much violence that fills much of the world. I was an actual immigrant and I was hoping for Lady Liberty to put her arms around me and my family, to receive us and eventually for us to become legal citizens. I was a thousand something miles from home, in the back of a pickup truck with four other strangers and we had made it across the Mexican/American border. We were exhausted and smelled really bad like sweat, smelly underarms, and the sweet stench of urine, and the Mexican sewer. We looked out of the window of the truck and the first thing I saw was the huge four lane highways with no pot holes at all. We all marveled at the size of everything, and how all was so neatly cared for. We arrived in San Antonio where we checked into a hotel. We all got cleaned up and showered leaving those bathtubs pretty disgusting. We changed into our clothes from our back packs and threw the dirty clothes away. The Coyotes surprised us with a buffet like dinner they had for us. They had food of all sorts; I remember there was fast food from just about everywhere. There were McDonald's Hamburgers, KFC Buckets of Chicken, Biscuits, Rolls, Coleslaw, and Mash Potatoes. There was Taco Bell, Burger King, and all types of sodas. We all ate a lot that day, and after that big buffet we all knew it was time to part our separate ways. We thanked the Coyotes for their help and they left us at the bus station. At the bus station we bought our tickets to our final destinations. The Mexican couple got their tickets to Chicago, and Claudia, Dario, and I were all heading towards New York City. We all said our goodbyes and took off. Three days later we were arriving in NYC, the Capital of the World. Silvio picked me up and took me to his home in Stratford, Connecticut. I thanked God that I had made it and that I was still alive.

Chapter Three

THE ILLEGAL IMMIGRANT

Hello Papa, how are you today? Hey son I'm good and you? I'm fine Dad, and I have good news for you. Oh really what is it? We're going to Colombia on vacation and I wanted to ask if we can stay with you? Of course you can son, that's great news! Yeah and I can interview you in person oh and I'm taking a tape recorder to record our conversations also. That's awesome son, I can't wait to see you! Now are you ready for your interview today? Yes I am son, just ask away. Ok, so after you got here, where were you living, and how did you make money? Alright when I got here, I arrived in Connecticut and was living with your uncle . . .

. . . .

Stratford was a nice size city with some work for people in my situation. Stratford was about an hour away from New York City, which I liked to visit a lot. I had arrived during the summer time and I quickly began looking for work everywhere. With no legal papers it was very difficult to find a job. Fall came around and it felt nice and cool, but 50 degrees was cold enough for me. I did get little jobs here and there but nothing that was going to help me pay back Silvio and bring my family here to be with me. The winter came and I couldn't believe how cold this planet could get! Everything was so cold and I really felt and believed that my fingers, ears, toes, and nose would just freeze and break off into little pieces! My fear of that happening would cause me to cover myself with a beanie, earmuffs, scarf, gloves, and double or triple socks on not including the normal sweater, jacket, and thick jeans, and work boots I wore to go to work. The local populace would look at me strange when they would see me as if they'd seen an alien. That was fine with me just as long as they didn't see an ILLEGAL ALIEN. The winters here made me want to hibernate and stay inside to keep warm. On the positive side, I saw snow for the first time and I loved it, its white color and the way it sounds and feels when you walk on it, I loved the crunching sound with the feeling of your feet sinking in it. The way snow made everything look was beautiful, but you tend to get tired of the snow very quickly. The snow covered everything and made it hard to get to work, and having to shovel snow off the doorway, driveway, sidewalk, and then having to dig your car out of the snow was absurd. This was usual for people here but this was amazing to me and I remember a few times that it had snowed so much that it covered the cars completely. Many times I was out shoveling snow, digging the car out and then realizing that I had dug out the neighbor's car by mistake. What the hell?! This was ridiculous! The upside to this was that sometimes the neighbors would dig out our car by mistake also. The winter was crazy up here. I still couldn't find a good job so I decided to move to New York City to look for better job opportunities.

It was 1978; I was living in New York City "The Capital of the World" with its tall, wide skyscrapers that filled the sky and pierced the clouds. I saw it all, from Rockefeller Center, to Broadway, The Empire State Building, The Statue of Liberty, and Time Square, it was all so awesome. Rock, Disco, and Salsa was heard coming from people's cars, from inside people's apartments, and in the neighborhoods. I loved listening to music because it calmed me down, and my problems didn't seem so bad. I could hear the music in the city, songs by The Eagles with Hotel California, The Police, Chicago with If you leave me now, Led Zeppelin with Stairway to Heaven, Janice Joplin, Blondie, James Brown, and so many more. I remember Disco giants The Bee gees with Night Fever, Staying Alive, and Disco Inferno. Hector Lavo, Willy Colon, Celia Cruz, Oscar De Leon, Tito Puente, Frankie Ruiz, and El Gran Combo were the Salsa Kings, and Queens. With all the Puerto Ricans, and all the other Latin Americans that lived in New York there was a high demand for these Salsa groups to play in the city. Studio 54 was still open when I lived in New York, but it shortly closed down due to all the problems it had in the early 70's. When I had some extra cash, I liked going to the movie theater. Movies at that time were Saturday Night Fever starring John Travolta, The Godfather, Rocky, and Animal House starring James Belushi, and Jaws was also playing in theaters. The 70's were groovy man, all I needed now was my family by my side and things would be great.

As for work in New York City I only found jobs that sucked, for the lack of a better word. Jobs like the sweeper, mopper, dishwasher, cleaner, painter, bus boy, the guy who takes out the trash, who cleans the toilets, the guy who gets called for clean up on isle 9 kind of jobs. Yes that was my life, I did all the jobs that most people did while in high school, and others didn't want to do. The good thing about that was I got to meet people from other Latin countries, like Puerto Ricans, Dominicans, Hondurans, Nicaraguans, Mexicans, Peruvians, Ecuadorians, more Colombians; Europeans like Italians, Spanish, Ukrainians, Russians, and others. Jobs were hard to find as an illegal alien, so I had to take whatever I could find. I lived in a small, ugly apartment in Brooklyn. It was so ugly and old that I thought the city inspectors would come and condemn it one day or that a door slamming would make it all come crashing down on top of us. The building had lots of immigrants living there, it seemed the walls were made from paper, and you could hear your neighbors as if they were in your apartment. Sexual relations was a comical attraction here; these private moments became a spectacle because you could hear the action on the whole floor, especially when there was moaning and groaning accompanied by the rhythmic banging and clanging of the aluminum frame bed. Mocking the couples' moaning seemed popular but then curse words followed really loud. "SHUT UP EFFERS!!! YOU SOB's!!!" When I thought that things couldn't get any more awkward than that, for some cosmic reason when payday weekend came around every couple in the building wanted to procreate and the symphony orchestra began to play. Banging here, clanging there, moaning then groaning! The walls shook the aluminum beds banged, it was too embarrassing to listen to. I thought, "The building is surely to collapse with this stress on the support columns!" I couldn't take the noise so I'd take the train to Manhattan for a walk. These days made me miss my wife extremely. Time square was amazing though and as I looked at the city lights I would think about her and hoped to have my family near me soon. I'd take a walk to give my neighbors enough time for them to go to sleep and by the time I'd get back the building would be nice and quiet. This apartment building had more problems other than this one, there were roaches too and I hate roaches. It was like the roaches were part of the lease, they lived here too but I couldn't get used to them trying to eat my food. No matter how many roaches you could kill in one day, there was more the next day, as if they multiplied when you stepped on them. It seemed like the cockroach community had gathered together and said, "Let's infest, and disgust Gilberto." I hated roaches more than ever, more than in Mexico where they tried to climb on me in the sewers, now they were climbing on me while I slept, YUUUUUUCK!!! Besides living in this ugly old apartment in one of the five boroughs of NYC, I also had to catch the subway to go to work; I had a part-time job at the docks catching and throwing fish where I only made enough money to pay for rent and barely take care of myself. I washed clothes in a coin laundry mat where I would take my clothes in a black garbage bag because I had nothing else to carry it in. Other than those little details, life was great. Sarcasm, yes my health was fine, I had a place to live, food in my belly when I needed it, and clothes on my back, but I was miserable. I missed my wife Piedad and my son, I missed my other family, and I even missed Colombia. All these new places I saw were great and the experiences I was living were educational, but without my wife and my son, I was very lonely. I could not call them because I could not afford a phone call since it was very expensive. All that we could do was write to each other, and I wrote Piedad a letter every few days. The mail took almost 2 weeks to receive meaning I had to try to remember what I wrote to her 2 weeks ago. I also would receive a letter every two days which helped me a lot, but not having them by my side was painful. I would visit my brother Silvio in Connecticut often and during the holidays. He was my only family nearby. I would talk and vent about my problems, and ask for advice, which was helpful in keeping me sane. That's what I did to pass my time, and keeping busy working also made me forget about my loneliness.

In the spirit of the 70's I had long black wavy hair, a very light complexion, I was tall and skinny, and had hazel green eyes. I also wore an earring on one of my ears so I blended in with the crowd. I looked good back then and I would have women hit on me a lot too. I was in my 20's and there was lots of temptation, sadly I fell to them and there had been a Puerto Rican woman that worked in the same place as I did that offered to marry me to give me my citizenship, but she wanted me to forget about my family in Colombia. I could not forget about Piedad and my son and the promise I made to them, so I turned her down and I felt horrible for almost taking the offer. I had a few jobs, and one of those jobs was in a factory. This job I liked, the hours were nice and the pay wasn't that bad either. After a few months of working there, I was able to save good money, and that made me feel good. But sometimes good things never last. I was working one day on the line when all of the sudden someone yelled at the top of their lungs, "La Migra!!!!" I thought it was a bad joke at first but everyone began running like chickens with their heads cut off. People began running for the exits, but some men from the outside began running in, flashing their badges and yelling at people to stop running. They identified themselves as Immigration. They said that all illegal workers were under arrest. "Oh my God, please get me out of this bad situation and don't let me get caught," I quickly thought in my head. There were other workers there that were Americans, and the boss simply told them to go home, so they grabbed their stuff and began leaving. I got this crazy idea; I calmly grabbed my jacket, slung it over my shoulder, and started walking out. I had to pass by a few officers but I kept cool although my heart was about to explode, I looked at one of them and nodded my head like what's up, and kept going. I walked out of the building with the others, but when I had reached the corner of the block I ran as fast as I could before someone gave me away. I had just evaded capture from immigration, I couldn't believe it! The immigration officers had arrested a lot of people and had their hands full, and I looked Caucasian almost so I got away. Needless to say I had to search for another job, and I remembered that Maria, Piedad's sister lived in New Jersey. I moved to New Jersey with Maria to see if I would have better luck there. Maria worked at a dry cleaner warehouse and she was able to get me a job there. I worked there for a while and was able to save more money. The boss didn't like me very much and would yell at me a lot. Until one day I got tired of his yelling and I yelled back, "SHUT YOUR DARN MOUTH AND STOP YELLING AT ME BEFORE I PUNCH YOU IN YOUR FACE!!!" I got in an argument with him where I called him everything in the book in English and in Spanish so I quit before he said you're fired. Yeah I was in my 20's and I had a very bad temper. I didn't take crap from anyone anymore after living such a bad childhood, and I was quick to blow up in people's faces, and even fighting. My search for another job began again, and I found myself moving to Rhode Island. There I found a good job and I kept my cool so I wouldn't get fired again. A year had passed, and fall was coming around again and I was tired of being far from my family. The winter approached again and I didn't even want to remember how miserable I was the winter before freezing my butt off with no one to come home to.

It had been almost two years; I had enough of working two to three jobs, living in crappy apartments, working for less than minimum wage, getting treated like dirt by the bosses, and worrying about getting caught by immigration. I was depressed and tired, and I was not thinking straight when I left everything and flew back to Colombia. It had taken me one day to get back home, when it took me almost a week to get across the Mexican border, I was insane for leaving. I had flown in without letting anybody know so they were surprised to see me and yes a little happy, but when they realized what I had done they quickly were upset with me. They were right though, I had quit and I had nothing to show for it, just a small savings. My brothers and sisters would call me a loser for leaving and they said not to count on them for any money to get back. I had been so depressed and just wanted to see my wife and my son that I didn't see the wrong that I had done.

Piedad was happy to see me but she agreed with the others about coming back with nothing. Ok I know that I was wrong but what was done is done, no turning back now. After all that drama all I could think about was getting to know my son, I hadn't seen him in two years, and he was almost three. Piedad worked and I got a job and we lived with Piedad's parents. It was not comfortable because it was a small house with three small rooms and at least six people lived there already.

I quickly remembered our living conditions and how poor we were, and that we would not have a bright future, not to mention what kind of future my son would have. I knew that I needed to get back to the United States, but I knew that my brothers and sisters would not help me anymore. I was going to need another miracle, so Piedad told me that we needed to pray for help. Now I had to believe that something would happen and put my faith at work. After a few months I was starting to feel that maybe God didn't hear me, but I kept working and I tried not to worry about it. As the months went by, one night my brother Joel the Colombian Marine called me upset and he sounded very nervous. "Hey Gilberto what's up?" "Nothing, here with the family, working and that's about it. Why, what's up with you, why do you sound nervous?" Joel then told me to meet up with him because he needed to talk to me urgently. I did as he said and took a bus to his neighborhood. When he opened the door he seemed nervous and told me to hurry inside. "Ok tell me what happened, because you're starting to worry me," I said. We sat down in the living room and he began telling me why he was so nervous. "Ok brother this is what happened. One day I went to pick up my wife from her friend's house, a Gipsy fortune teller, my wife told me that her friend wanted to read my fortune one day." "So what did you say?" I asked. "It's a long story so just listen ok" he sounded irritated. "I told the lady that I was not interested but she insisted and was very convincing, so I said ok. Later that week I met up with her at her house. Now I'm thinking this lady was going to pull out her crystal ball and make strange faces while she read my fortune but she was very normal. She began by doing a little chant then held my hands and looked at them. She pulled out her Terra cards and started shuffling them around. She pulled out cards and told me that I was going to have a huge change in my life. She asked me if I had any enemies, but I was stunned by the question and I said no. She pulled out more cards and told me that I was going to get in a huge gun fight. My heart skipped a beat and then pounded on my chest! What do you mean?! I asked her but she continued and said that I would get into a shootout and that someone was going to get shot. I began sweating and my mind was searching for any possible enemies that I could have. I could not think of any while she continued, she smiled and put her hand on mine and said that it wouldn't be me. That was a relief but it still made me nervous to think that I was going to shoot someone, especially someone that I did not know. I was pale and asked her when this would happen, but she just said before the year is over. She told me that I was going to travel to a faraway place and that my life would dramatically change. She told me not to worry but to be careful and finished her session. I walked out of her house shaking and still thinking of any possible enemies. The following weeks were a blur and I could not focus at work because of it, so I decided to forget about the whole story and told myself that it was nothing but bullcrap! My life was normal and I got back into my groove. One normal day I picked up my wife Nora from work and we drove home. We drove into the garage parking lot underneath the apartment building and I was parking my car in reverse. As we parked the car and as soon as I turned it off, I heard a loud **BANG!** My front windshield had a hole in it from a gunshot! Nora and I ducked from the loud noise but when I looked out the windshield I saw the shooter! It was a former friend of mine that I had borrowed money to. He had not paid me back and we had argued about the money, he did threaten me once but I thought it was just out of anger. I realized that day that he was dead serious! He shot again and this time he was trying to shoot at my head but it missed. I grabbed Nora and pushed her head under the dashboard as I reached for my revolver. She was screaming as the shots kept coming through the windshield, the glass shattered into pieces and we were showered by little glass squares. I opened my door and jumped out of the car, shielding myself with my door and I ran behind the other cars to create distance from the shooter and to get him away from Nora. I was using the other cars in the garage as cover. Loud pops, the sound of bullets zipping in the air, followed by car glass shattering echoed in the car garage. He had two pistols, one in each hand, as his bullets finished he reloaded his magazine and kept shooting at me. I only had a revolver carrying six bullets so at first I shot as he shot to keep him away, but he was getting closer. I shot my last bullet and just heard "click, click" and it seemed louder than the bang of the bullets, but remembered that I had extras in my glove box. I quickly ran to my car, grabbed more bullets, and ran away from my car again while he was reloading both guns and was hiding behind a cement pillar so he did not see me go get more bullets. He began shooting again and I returned fire but this time conserving my shots. I began aiming better instead of just having wild shots. This guy got closer as I moved from car to car getting further from him. I was at my last shot again and I stopped shooting. He noticed that I stopped and he ran closer to me but I saw him and got behind a car and waited for him. He must have thought that I was out of bullets and he stuck his head out from around the corner where I was waiting. When I saw his head pop out from that corner I took my shot, **bang**! He hit the ground like a sack of potatoes. I had shot him in the head and I ran up to him as he lay on the ground bleeding from his face. I shot more at his head but heard, "click, click, click" and remembered that I had no more bullets. I was so furious about him trying to kill me that I had tried to shoot him more. My anger was calmed and turned into fear thinking that I had just shot a man in the head and if he wasn't dead already that he could possibly die from the wound and that I would be going to prison. I jumped back in my car and drove off as fast as I could. Nora was so scared that she had peed all over herself. Since then I have been laying low. I found out that the man is still alive but can't talk right and is still in the hospital. Now I have serious consequences to face. I talked to my lawyers but they say that the prosecutor wants me to do some jail time. All the witnesses that were there say I reacted in self-defense but I still don't understand the prosecutor's decision." I could not believe what my brother Joel had just told me. He wanted me to take care of his family while he laid low in another city.

 Joel was keeping a low profile and wanted to leave town. He had applied for a travel visa for the U.S. a while ago but it hadn't been approved yet. He was waiting for the approval for him and his family to leave Colombia, and now he needed it sooner, he didn't want to leave his family alone and risk them getting hurt or killed from revenge. Lucky for him after two months his visa was approved, but not for his wife or daughter. Poor guy was real desperate and needed to take them with him, but the only solution was to get them through the border. Going through Mexico was extremely dangerous and to send his wife and daughter alone was crazy. By this time there were other ways to get into the United States, and through the Bahamas was one of those other ways. By boat sounded much easier so he decided to send them but he did not want to send them alone, he needed someone he could trust. Joel said to me, "I know that you want to get back to 'La USA' and I need someone I can trust to get my wife and daughter over the border through the Bahamas, through El Hueco." When he asked me, I couldn't believe it, my miracle was happening. "I will cover your flights and other transportation and you can repay me some other day, alright Gilberto." "Yes!" I said, "of course anything to help a brother out." We planned our trip and we packed because this needed to happen quickly. Joel heard that the law was looking for him. The plan was to go to the Bahamas by plane, Joel would continue to Miami, and I would help his wife, Nora and daughter get into Miami by boat. In Miami we had a sister living there with her husband, where we all planned to meet each other.

The day came where we were saying goodbye to everyone at the airport. I was only in Colombia for 8 months before I was leaving for the States again, what a miracle! We flew out of Colombia to Quito, Ecuador, and then we flew to the Bahamas. A few hours later we were landing in Nassau, Bahamas. As soon as we landed on the runway, we began saying our goodbyes to Joel. He had a few words with his family and hugged them. Then he told me to take care of his family. "I'll treat them as if they were my own." I said. He hugged us all and wished us luck. The plane stopped and we had to get off. He and his wife had tears in their eyes, and his daughter, only 3 at the time, was sobbing. They were scared for the unexpected road ahead of us, but since I had been through once already I wasn't that nervous. We exited the plane into Nassau International Airport; we got our luggage, something to eat, and then planned on getting a hotel for the night. It was dark already when we left the airport; we got a cab and drove to the cheapest hotel around since we didn't have much money to play with. There we rested and went to bed quickly because we had a busy schedule the next day. That night I woke up to a noise at the door, "what's going on?" I asked myself. Nora then said in a scared whisper, "there's someone trying to get in!" I jumped out of bed and ran to the door, where I rammed my shoulder against the door and yelled as loud as I could in English, "who the hell is it!" I heard two men shouting as they ran away. The yell plus the ramming of the door must have scared them away. "What the hell was that?!" we said to ourselves. I think someone was trying to get in to rob us or something. I locked the door again and this time we barricaded it with furniture in case the thieves tried again. We tried to go back to sleep but it was harder now from what had occurred. When morning came we got ready and got our stuff, and while we were checking out I mentioned what had happened. The ladies at the counter apologized and said it could have been local thieves trying to rob tourists, and that unfortunately it wasn't the first time this kind of thing happened. Nora and Katy were so glad that I was with them on this trip after what had happened to us. We left and we had to take a boat to the last island closest to Miami, which is Bimini. When we arrived we looked around the docks for those planning to take people across. I bargained for a cheaper boat ride and I spoke broken English so it worked out nice. There were local boat owners and American boat owners at the docks making easy money. A grand or two for a boat ride to America, and the immigrants paid for the gas, too easy. I began my bargaining with the Americans, I trusted them more than the locals after last night. I spoke my broken English as best as I could, I through in the "F" word occasionally to build some rapport with them. I made them laugh and I was able to negotiate our cost. For us three, one bag, plus the gas, we had to pay $2,400, not bad. At nightfall there were cops all around the docks because there had been some shooting involving drug smugglers and the police earlier that day so our trip was cancelled. The next night we took off for Miami but an hour into the trip we had to turn around; a heavy storm had caused the waves to get so high that it denied us a safe boat ride. A few days later after the storm had passed we tried again and this time it was a go. Now that we had our boat ride, we had to get all our clothes in one bag; we ate, and had to wait for nightfall to give us concealment from the Coast Guard. Once it was dark enough, we jumped into the boat, which was at least a 27ft boat big enough for at least ten. But to keep from looking too suspicious there was us three and another, together with the two guys driving made it six. They had fishing poles for us all and made us wear life vests and told us that we had to pretend that we had been fishing. We all had to play the roles in case we were stopped by the authorities. Pretty clever I thought, but hoped that our acting debuts would not come that night. The Americans filled the boat with some gas and we were off. The water was not too choppy that night so we were having a smooth ride. There was nothing but darkness ahead of us, and behind us was the sound of the waves hitting the shore, getting fainter as we got farther. You could see some lights from some houses off the small island, but that was it. Soon we couldn't see any more lights just the crescent moon smiling down at us, and we could see all the stars. Katy said, "Uncle I can see all the stars," we all agreed with her, it was beautiful. Everyone was quiet looking at the moon and the stars. The only noises out there were the boat's engines humming, and the sound of waves hitting the boat. All those factors and the smell of the ocean made it very peaceful. The long ride gave us lots of time to think and imagine all sorts of things. I thought of having my family come through this way since it looked easier. I wish I would have come this way before and it would have saved me from the sewer crawl in Mexico. It had been a couple of hours and we began seeing the lights coming from Miami's downtown. Little by little we began seeing the buildings, and then as we got closer, the city got bigger and bigger. The Americans turned off one engine and ran the other at low speed not to appear in such a hurry. We all were anxious to get to shore and the speed of the boat was torture for us all. Finally we made it to the beach, "Get off the boat!"

the Americans shouted. We jumped off into the shallow water on the beach and quickly made it off the beach into some neighborhood of beach houses. Luckily it was late enough that there were no people out, because it would have been weird trying to explain why we were wet and dragging a wet, sandy suitcase. We walked into the downtown area where we waved a taxi down. A taxi stopped and picked us up, and when the driver saw that we were wet and sandy, he asked in Spanish with a Cuban accent, "Vienen de Cuba?" (Coming from Cuba?) I talked to the taxi driver, who told me that he had come from Cuba by boat some years ago. He dropped us off at my sister's house, and we were happy to have made it with no problems at all. We walked up the porch and Katy rang the doorbell. "Who is it?" Delma asked, "Its Nora, Katy, and Gilberto." We answered. We could hear Delma calling Joel and her husband and telling them that we were at the door. They unlocked the door's many locks and finally opened the door, but then had to open the gate over the door. That's the way houses look in Miami, with gates over the windows and doors giving them a nice prison feel. Joel came out and hugged his family and helped us in. Delma and her husband, Jorge had some mattresses for us to sleep on. They gave us dry clothes and put our wet clothes to wash. They received us very kindly and made us feel at home. Jorge had his own business in Miami, he actually owned a gate making business, and they lived comfortable. We told our story on how our trip went while we ate; that was a good night. After the nice warm greeting that night we went to sleep peacefully.

The next day came and I stepped outside to take a better look at Miami, I quickly loved the weather. It was warm, not like the freezing weather of New York and Connecticut. From what I had seen the night before, its downtown was nice too, meaning that there could be good chances for work. Now because Miami was the farthest south in the States, that meant there were more Latin Americans here too. I thought maybe Miami would be a better place to live, so I stayed at my sister's house and got a job in Miami. I was sleeping in the living room because there was no more room since my brother was here with his family too. This was just temporary until I had enough money to move out on my own. It was a very uncomfortable situation living there because the house was overcrowded and people were on the edge and irritable with each other. After a few months the tension was so thick that it caused an argument between my sister and I and she kicked me out. I didn't know anybody in Miami and had nowhere to go. I left with the little clothes I had and started walking the street now homeless and I didn't know what to do. I was angry and scared and I walked to a phone booth with the little money I had and I called my brother in Connecticut and told Silvio what happened. Silvio told me that his current wife had friends and family in Tampa, which was like 5 hours from Miami. Silvio told me to go to Tampa and to stay at his father-in-laws until I got a place of my own. I quickly got on a bus to Tampa, and this nice man called Don Adan picked me up. The Don is Mister in Spanish out of respect, but nothing to do with Mafia jargon. Tampa, Florida was a calm, nice, and small city with a bay on the Gulf of Mexico. I liked it, the Latin community was small so immigration was not common, and work was easy to find. I got a job and began saving money to bring Piedad and my son here. Don Adan was kind enough to let me stay until that was possible. Unfortunately by then Silvio had gotten a divorce from his wife and was tired of the bitter cold winters and came down to Tampa also. He was a smart, talented guy and got a good job real quick. He rented an old wooden house off of Florida Ave, and asked me to move in with him so I did. After almost a year I had saved enough money to bring my family here. I sent Piedad the money and told her to come through the Bahamas since it had been so easy for me and my brother's family. Our dreams were beginning to come true, and soon I was going to have my family with me.

The time came when Piedad and my son were at the airport in Colombia ready to come to "La USA!" I told Piedad to call me as soon as they arrived at my sister's in Miami; after that call I would not talk to them for two days until they called me from Miami. I had to work because I couldn't just leave to Miami and wait for them. It would take two days but they were going to feel like the longest days of my life. I tried to work and keep my mind busy but I couldn't stop thinking about all the dangers that Piedad and Paul could face. I would remember when I was with them in Colombia, how happy I was by their side and I didn't know what I would do without them. I remembered when I would take Paul to the airport in Pereira to watch the airplanes take off. There was a playground at the airport where I would put Paul on the swings, and soon I would take Paul to a playground here in Tampa. The first day went by and I could hardly sleep, and now the next day came. Hopefully by nightfall my family would be in Miami. The day at work was difficult and I was stressed out, constantly looking at the time but that darn clock would not move. It was dark out and I was going home but was so anxious to get that call so I could relax. I tried to go to sleep but all I did was toss and turn in the mattress on the floor where I slept. When at last the phone began ringing and it woke me up. I quickly answered it, and I heard Piedad's voice. She had made it to Miami and called me from my sister's house. "Hola Papi!" both Piedad and Paul said to me. They had made it safe and now I had to drive to Miami to pick them up. I drove into Miami that same night and was knocking at my sister's house later in the dark morning hours. I was so happy to see them here, and now we were finally together. We sat down and Piedad told me about their trip. Piedad said "Honey, after we last spoke when I was in Colombia I bought the plane tickets and the next day we flew to Ecuador, there was a large group of women and some with children going through "El Hueco" into Miami. We talked and I decided to tag along with their group. Then we flew into the Bahamas where we got a Hotel and kept with the group. On the following day we took small boat rides to Bimini and there's where we paid to get to Miami by boat. There were probably 10 women and some small children on the boat with us. We left at night and arrived in Miami Beach around 12am where we all jumped into the water and began walking to the shore. But at that same moment when our boat sped away a Police helicopter showed up with a bright light shining down on the beach. All of us women with our children hid behind bushes as the helicopter flew around shining their light making us all very nervous. We were thinking the worst while it flew around, would we be arrested and sent back home what do we do? But then it flew away just like that. We all quickly ran to the road and waved down taxis to get away fast before Police arrived. I took a taxi with four other women and arrived here at your sisters. The other ladies called their families here in Miami and were picked up soon after, and here we are." They had made it safe and I thanked God and was very grateful that we were finally together here in the United States. This all happened the fall of October 1980.

Chapter Four

TOGETHER AGAIN

Wow son this is so awesome to have you and your mom right here with me today. I know Dad, and hopefully we can all be together again like when Michael and I were kids. Paul did you ever bring that tape recorder with you? Yes I did and tomorrow we can begin alright.

The very next day after breakfast: Alright Papa, it's time for business, you ready? Sure thing son ask me your questions. Last time we spoke we were all together again, do you remember? Yes that's when I was the happiest man alive . . .

. . . .

We were living in Tampa, Florida and the year was 1980. Piedad, Paul, and I were living in Silvio's house, and we three lived in one room. We didn't have any furniture, we only had one mattress where Paul slept on and we slept on the floor. Now that we had a place to live, Piedad had to find a job. She had been using a sewing machine since she was a young girl to fix her clothes or make her own clothes. She quickly found a job as a seamstress and I had a job as a waiter. As time went by we were able to buy our own things, furniture, clothes, silverware, etc . . . We lived with Silvio for a while but a few years later my brother Juan also came to the States by via Mexico and he moved in with all of us too. We decided to get our own place to have more privacy and moved into a mobile home off Sheldon Road. Tampa was a small city and we sometimes got the evil eye or would get called: Wetbacks, Spicks, and Lat'nos, but I just learned to ignore people like that and be positive. Besides I did have some good American friends also and you can't judge all by a few.

Our income was not that great but we were happy being together and we made it work. We moved around a lot because after the first year the rent would go up and we couldn't afford it, it also kept immigration guessing. We tried to make the best of things and occasionally we would go on trips to the beautiful Florida beaches of Clearwater, St Pete, and Sarasota. We also went to the Natural Springs, like Lithia Springs in Brandon or Crystal Springs near Ocala. We made friends that were in the same situation as us, and they were mostly Colombian people. There was a large community of Cubans in Ybor City, and Mexican migrant workers in Brandon, but we lived on the other side of town, Town and Country to be specific. Colombian people were rare, so we were a close group. We would get together and have parties, or go on trips; it was a nice life. The 80's were here and the big names heard on the radio were: Michael Jackson, The Rolling Stones, Bruce Springsteen, Pat Benatar, Phil Collins, Elton John, Billy Crystal, George Michael, and in Latin music I listened too Oscar De Leon from Venezuela, El Gran Combo and Frankie Ruiz from Puerto Rico, Ruben Blades from Panama, and Celia Cruz from Cuba. The Star Wars and Superman Movies were playing in theaters. Years were going by fast and Paul began going to school. In 1982 Piedad became pregnant again. We were very happy about having kids but it was stressful thinking if we would be able to afford another child or not. Piedad was expecting a boy and we started looking for names again. Piedad and I could not decide on a name for our boy but one day we asked Paul what names he liked. Paul answered and said, "My friend's name is Michael and I like Michael Jackson too." It was decided then, we thought that it was a nice strong American name for a boy so our boy's name would be Michael. Michael was born in August and he was born a Citizen of the United States, what a blessing for him that he would not have to struggle to get his legal papers or face the constant threat of deportation. We were a family of four now and we were beginning to live a little better. The first few years had gone by quickly and we were so excited to be together again. The satisfaction of not having anything and buying our things little by little was a great accomplishment. Also when we would send money to our family in Colombia that made us feel great and all the hard work and sacrifice was worth it.

  In the mid 80's there was an economic recession where it made it hard for us to make a living. I decided to move the family to Miami where there were better job opportunities and better pay. With all our clothes packed tightly into boxes, all our furniture stacked up high in the U-Haul we began our road trip south on Interstate 75. Almost five hours later we reached Interstate 95 and kept going south. The highways began to grow larger and looked like tangled up spaghetti the way they twisted and turned around one another, and no matter how large the road got it didn't stop the traffic from getting backed up. The sound of car horns filled the streets followed by loud insults with those hand signals that angered the receivers. The buildings replaced trees, the peace and quiet was gone, and we knew right away that we were in a real city. Miami was 10 times bigger than Tampa, was definitely more expensive and traffic was insane. The bigger the city, the more problems it had, crime was really high, and more accidents due to the traffic and the heat with the rain made Miami seem like a giant sauna. We quickly noticed that in Miami people's clothes got skimpier, bodies were in better shape, and people got tanner. It looked like the city was filled with darn swimsuit models or something. While we were seeing everything so nice we thought that this move would be great for us, but then we drove past all the nice neighborhoods and arrived in Hialeah where it didn't look so nice. We rented a small apartment and it was a decent place to live; besides my sister lived a half hour away in Miami which we could visit at any time to get out of Hialeah.

We were situated and we began job hunting and found jobs quickly. Piedad as a seamstress and I found work at the Marriot near downtown. It was a five star hotel where I was a waiter in their fancy restaurant. But in Miami I discovered a different world, a world of luxury, of the rich and famous. I would get assigned to work on the big banquets in the hotel. The banquets and parties that were held by these people were outrageously rich; it was a life to envy. These people would drop hundreds of dollars buying bottles of wine and liquor, caviar and other gourmet foods that I couldn't pronounce. I met all types of rich people and sometimes celebrities. They always seemed to like me for some reason, and I liked having conversations with them. One ordinary night out of so many nights working a banquet, a guest at the party liked the way I worked and began a conversation with me. "So what's your name friend?" I answered, "My name is Gilberto." "I can hear an accent, so where are you from?" Since we were in Miami, and Miami was saturated with Cubans, he asked. "Are you Cuban?" "Oh I'm from Colombia." "Colombia!" He said. "Yeah I hear that place is beautiful and that lots of Cocaine is grown there. Is that true man?" "Yes Colombia is beautiful and rich with all plants and wildlife, but the Coca also grows there." "So all you Colombians have Cocaine growing everywhere? You guys must throw some crazy parties! Hahaha." But I said, "No in Colombia most people are poor, and only the Drug Smugglers grow it and ship it here, but it is illegal there too." Then the man said, "Well illegal or not, I love that Colombian Yeyo ha ha ha," and he laughed again. "Hey Gilberto, have you ever had any?" "No I don't do that." "Do you wanna try some?" "No thank you." "So you're telling me that Colombia has all that Coke, and you have never tried any?" he said, then I said in a joking manner, "Look we Colombians are business men, and we sell a product to you Gringos, who pay good money to get messed up, so we in return could live good lives!" Everyone that was listening to our conversation began laughing hysterically. The guy said to me with a big smile on his face, "Gilberto you are a very funny man, and I like you. My name is Rich, and if you ever need anything, let me know, ok." "Ok thanks Rich, it was nice meeting you too." "Oh by the way Gilberto, do you know anyone who sells the stuff? I'm running low and would like to have more dealers to provide for the demand." "No I don't know anyone." so I thought. This evil seed was planted, the thought had entered my mind, and I began to feel curious about this lifestyle. I could sell cocaine and make so much money that I could live like one of these people. Taking Piedad and the kids to fancy hotels and throwing expensive parties would be great. Taking trips around the world, and things like that filled my mind. Alright, I had to get back to the party and my feet had to land back on Earth. I am going to be honest the thought made me very excited. That night went well and I made real good tips from those rich people. But after the conversation with the gringo named Rich who was extremely rich opened my eyes to this trendy business that was exploding. I had a flashback of the news back in Colombia about the Coca plants. I was still innocent to all this and never had thought about it. Yes I knew that cocaine was a drug from South America and that people sold it and made lots of money, but I never had seen it so close in my life. I noticed that in the restaurant business there was lots of drug use and even drug dealers, but I never wanted any part of that life.

The movie Scar Face had hit theaters and people were getting more familiar with this drug. "Yeyo" was the popular name for it and I saw this lifestyle become a fashion overnight, it seemed like every Colombian or Latin American wanted to get involved in selling drugs. Everyone wanted to be Tony Montana. With the God Father Movies out too it started all the Mafia crazes. Yes the Mafia existed before those movies but it seemed like after these movies came out, people just wanted to live those sorts of lives. I found out that my sister's husband had cousins that had been selling the stuff for years, and needless to say they had lots of money, businesses, and expensive things. I even had a cousin in Miami, his name was Antonio, and he was selling cocaine too. He was the typical Miami Vice stereo-type bad guy, wearing those crazy hot pink shirts, or fluorescent colors with the big shirt collars, and the white pants, with the white snake leather shoes. He had the fancy house, with the clothes, the expensive button shirts with the first few unbuttoned showing off his hairy chest. He had gold chains hanging from his neck, a gold watch on his wrist, and with big gold rings on just about every finger. His wife and son had expensive stuff, everything nice and new. His son had toys that both Paul and Michael wanted to play with all the time and Paul would say, "Papi Lets go to Antonio's house." Antonio had an awesome jeep that I wanted to play with too. It was a life of luxury that everyone dreamed of having, but it was all illegal. I asked Antonio about the cocaine business and how good business was. Antonio told me, "Look Gilberto, this business is booming and you should jump on this man! It's not as dangerous like in Colombia, and here you make more money because you make it in dollars. If you keep your nose clean, no pun intended, and don't use your own product, you don't steal from your supplier or are short on your part, and you keep your mouth shut if cops catch you, you'll be safe." "Wow don't you think that's a lot of Ifs? What about if one of those goes wrong then they send you the guys on motorcycles?" (This term, guys on the motorcycles meant hit men, also known as Sicarios.) Antonio said, "Look man those people that you hear about getting killed on the news, like that one massacre at that Mall, uhh, The Dadeland Mall Massacre in 1979 by those Sicarios was because of competition. The big bosses here were losing money because some other greedy idiots wanted it for themselves; it's a war between us the Colombians and the Cubans. But people like you and me only want to make a little, just enough to make our lives a little better but not enough to bother anyone big. You know what I mean?" "Yeah I guess I know what you mean but I still think it's too risky, what about if you get caught, what will happen?" He said, "The police here still don't really know about this business and jail time is real short. There are no real laws against it and hope there will never be, because I'm making a fortune man. You know that I made $3,000 this last month, not to mention my own income. I have my job where I have benefits and report taxes to keep the IRS away, and I make like an average of $750 a week extra just by receiving this stuff, taking it, and distributing it to others, that's all. I am not the drug dealer that you see in the corners of the neighborhood but a classy type of business man." "I see, so have you ever gotten caught?" "No man, but if so I always keep my stuff in someone else's house, that's the secret. So if they catch me, they won't find it all and you don't get in that much trouble." "I see, alright Antonio thanks for the info cousin. Take care." He then asked, "So do you want in or what man?" "No thanks man, I don't think I need that kind of trouble in my life." My conversation with Antonio was educational and very tempting, but I did not want trouble with the gringos. A few months passed after our conversation and my brother Juan got arrested back in Tampa. It was like I asked Antonio what could happen if someone got caught and Juan got arrested for selling cocaine. He went to trial and was sentenced to 3 years. We went to visit him in a state prison somewhere in Florida. When we saw him, he was in his light blue jumpsuit with a number on his back that all inmates wore and we sat down with him in the visitors' area. "So tell us what happened, why did you get arrested?" I asked, because no one really knew that he had been selling drugs. He told us what happened but in Spanish and so nobody else could hear the conversation. Juan said, "So I was selling the merchandise along with Fernando to friends, and friends of theirs. We were making all sorts of serious cash, but somehow the cops found out and they went to our apartment to arrest us, both me and Fernando. We were just getting home from being in the street, and we saw the cops knocking on our door. It was a drug bust, they were dressed with helmets and vests with Police written on them, and had shotguns. As soon as we saw that, Fernando slammed on the brakes, which caught their attention. The cops started yelling at us to get out, with shotguns and pistols pointing at us, but Fernando put it in reverse and sped out of there in a hurry. The cops jumped in their cars and began chasing us." We all could not believe what he was saying. "Are you crazy Juan?!" My sister yelled at him. "Anyway we were getting chased by about three cars, two cop cars, and an unmarked car. The chase lasted a few minutes with us trying to get away at high speeds, but we knew that it was not gonna happen. In one instance Fernando tried to take a turn going too fast but the car spun out of control and crashed inside a ditch. We were okay but really dizzy, and when we looked around us the cops had surrounded the truck. They pulled us out, through us on the ground, and cuffed us. There were some drugs in the car so we were charged with possession of illegal drugs and eluding law enforcement." We talked some more and gave him hope that hopefully the time would go by fast. Juan served less than three years and got out early for good behavior.

Back in Miami my life with Piedad was not good, the stress level was high and my attitude was getting bad, there were lots of fights because I worked a lot and hardly saw her and the kids. It was hectic, and people were so rude. We were poor, had very little, and Miami was an expensive place. People didn't want us around them and we felt the neglect. I could compare it to walking on the Hollywood Red Carpet dressed poorly and getting torn alive by the critics. We also were living in Miami in the era of the Marielitos. If you know Miami history or you've seen Scar Face, you should know that the Marielitos was when Fidel Castro took all his worst criminals, the people from mental hospitals, and the people from Cuban slums and sent them on boats to Miami. In Scar Face this is one of the boats that Tony Montana came on. It was also the era of the Colombian Cocaine explosion in Miami. There was Cocaine in the night clubs and parties, and the U.S. Dollar bill had the constant tendency of rolling up on its own from where the previous owner had used it to snort the white powder. It was normal to find cocaine residue on dollar bills from where someone used it for that. It was normal to see car chases or hear shootouts and to hear about several murders a night on the news. Miami was ranked the most dangerous place to live in during these early years in the 80's because of the drug wars. I remember a day in our apartment complex where a car came out speeding from the parking lot with a young Hispanic man holding on to the hood of the car yelling at the drivers. The same apartments that my son Paul found a box of bullets or where there would be shell casings from spent bullets, or to see bullet holes on stucco houses where there was a shootout in a neighborhood. Miami life was crazy, one day Piedad and the kids were at a laundry mat where the ice cream parlor next door caught on fire and the man next door came into the laundry mat with his clothes burning and smoking, yelling to get out quickly because there was a fire next door. Thank God and to Fire Fighters our clothes did not burn but the clothes had to be washed again because they smelled like smoke. Miami Vice the show on TV was popular because people could relate to the action on the show. This was a crazy time for Miami and I did not want to live here anymore. After two and a half years, we decided to move back to Tampa, where we ended up living on a street called Church St. I thought it was a good sign.

Tampa was so much more relaxed and a humble place to live compared to the hectic life in Miami, I liked Tampa a lot, and it became our home. Paul was enrolled into school and Michael was still only 2 years old. I got my old job back as a waiter at a Spanish Restaurant, I didn't make as much as I did in Miami but it was much calmer, and people were much nicer than the rude snobs back in Miami. The family would get together at Silvio's house for holidays and Silvio was married again so there were bigger family reunions now. We would have great big parties and everyone would dance and was happy together. The winters in Florida were much colder than they are now, and everyone had to wear coats and jackets in the winter. I looked around at my family and I was happy, but for some reason I still thought about that talk with Rich and my cousin Antonio back in Miami. I thought about all their luxuries and I wanted some of that for me and my family. The holidays were here then gone and it was back to work again. I worked as a waiter at a local restaurant and I would make descent money, but I worked real hard and long hours standing, walking, and carrying things getting bossed around by the customers and of course the boss. I loved watching movies but sometimes there were movies that made me feel angry at my situation. I would see these rich people with great jobs having more and worrying less. At work I saw the same thing and I envied the American citizen. How could I become a boss, or a successful lawyer, banker or business man if I was not a legal citizen? Neither I nor my family would ever be that person in our situation, we needed to become citizens, but first I needed to become a legal resident. The opportunity eluded me and it made me angry. How could I become a legal resident, how long was it going to take, was it going to happen? Would Piedad and Paul have the opportunities that Michael was going to have as a citizen born here? The thought would torture me constantly. But life would go on as the illegal immigrants in Tampa. I shared my dilemma with Silvio but he had been authorized to come here so he had the chance to become a legal citizen one day. Now that Juan had been released from state prison he was back in Tampa. While he was locked up he read lots of books and grew a little smarter. Juan had come to the States the same way I did so we would talk and vent about our illegal immigrant problem. He was very intelligent and started going to college a few nights a week just to get an education but really not for a career because illegals are not able to have certain jobs here in the states. We brainstormed on how to overcome these huge obstacles in our way but many times our conversations ended with us knowing it was about chance and having lots of money when the chance came. Piedad and I agreed to file for legal residency with immigration but feared rejection and deportation. That would be devastating for us because we did not have any savings at all. The process of filing for legal residency with immigration was not only expensive but it was a process that would take numerous hours and entire days waiting in line at the immigration office. Once the papers would get filed with immigration it could still take months for them to approve those papers and the possibility of being rejected was very depressing. I can remember days where we would be at the immigration office before they were open and be there all afternoon just to ask certain questions or give them certain forms they needed. These were a few of our problems as illegal immigrants. Other problems were: not being able to have a good job, no health benefits, no retirement or pension, no vacations, no help from social services, fear of being arrested and deported, fear of getting fired and being homeless and hungry, and fear of getting sick with no money. I would tell Piedad and the kids all the time not too get sick or hurt because we had no money for Doctors. As if anyone could control their health or unforeseen accidents. There was so much fear that it was very difficult to really be happy. We had to be very careful and avoid all these problems. But because employers knew that illegal immigrants had so many fears, most of them would take advantage of us and exploit us by not paying the normal wages, longer hours, harder work, and they would then save on paying less and not having to report certain things on taxes. It was a huge business for many to hire illegals and make huge profits in return. They knew that illegal immigrants would never say a word and risk losing their jobs or getting deported. Piedad and I were saving money in case something like that would happen to us.

I began noticing the Miami trend make it to Tampa, more and more people were beginning either to sell drugs or use drugs, and it was a lucrative business. My brother Juan came to live with us for a while till he got back on his feet. I was curious about something so I asked him the question that I had inside for a while, but I made sure that Piedad was not around to hear us. "So Juan, I just need to ask you. How was the business when you were in and how much were you making?" Juan laughed, "Ha ha ha, do you want to do the same Gilberto?" "I'm just asking brother." I said. Juan replied, "Ok I'll tell you, it was nice man. I'm not gonna lie, I would make more money in one night than I could make in a week! All of the sudden you become the popular guy and everyone wants to be your friend. When you have money people become friendlier especially the hot women!" "Really?" I asked. "Yeah, well I always had hot women around me but now there were more, ha ha ha!" "Ok Casanova, so how did you get into this?" I asked him. "Fernando and I had met some Colombian dude that asked us if we were interested in making some extra cash, tax free. He must have seen the poor look on our faces, so we quickly told him sure thing, what do we do? And this guy got our numbers, we met later somewhere else and he told us that all we had to do was be delivery boys, that we would receive a package from one guy and give to another guy somewhere else. That seemed easy enough, so we said yes." I asked, "So how much did you guys make?" His eyes opened wide and he said, "In a year or so that we did this, we made an extra $45,000.00 each!" My jaw dropped and my heart began pounding, I could not believe the amount of money that he did. "So what did you do with it?" I asked. Juan said "I spent some of it on parties and things, and some on lawyers, but I saved the most of it and invested." "Where did you get the idea to invest from?" I asked, and he replied with a grin on his face, "From when I read books in jail and in college." We both laughed at his response but I felt scared in my heart from the consequences. He gave me so much information on how to keep a low profile, to keep it secret from others and how to avoid getting caught with the merchandise. He talked about the business as if it were legal and how we were just business men trying to make a profit. That the government was the monster that controlled everyone and kept us all weak and poor and had us making them rich by having to pay so much taxes on everything. He had learned all this from the other so-called business men that believed this so strongly in their hearts that it justified their actions. Juan had been secretly selling in small amounts so nobody would notice and he was saving tons of money to leave the country and be rich somewhere else. He asked me to think about it and to think about all the possibilities and the consequences. He did not want to pressure me into this and he told me that he understood if I did not want to do this because I had a family and he didn't. I appreciated his concern and his sincerity but now I had a major decision to make.

It was 1986 and Ronald Reagan was President. He had been talking about an Immigration Reform Act, it was written to control illegal immigrants from coming here but the IRCA also provided a program for certain illegal immigrants who had lived in the United States since January 1, 1982, to apply to become legal residents with the right to work. This was great news for all of us; this gave us the chance to become Residents and eventually to become Citizens of the United States of America. Ronald Reagan had signed the Immigration Reform and Control Act of 1986 in November and we through a party to celebrate this great day. Piedad and I went the following week to the immigration office to show that we qualified for the Reform Act. Now you can imagine after the news the immigration offices were so packed and busy with people from everywhere. After hours of waiting the Immigration Officer showed us how much it was going to cost for the three of us, we almost fell out of our chairs. It was not cheap but as soon as we had the money, all we had to do was pay and wait to receive our Legal Residency. We had been saving just in case our residency papers were rejected and we would have to leave to Colombia so we used that money and paid for the immigration papers. The process was not long after and we were given things to study for a test. It had American History and Political Science questions that we had to answer in order to get our Legal Residency. A few months later we were interviewed, took the test, and were told that we would receive our papers in the mail. We became Legal Residents of the United States, and this was a mile stone in our lives, a great accomplishment. Now with our legal papers we would be able to become Citizens of the United States and travel abroad, but when I asked when we would be eligible for Citizenship they told us after six years of being Legal Residents without any crimes committed. Wow, that seemed like an eternity for me. Six Years was a long time to wait for better jobs and better benefits. Well ok whatever I guess that's what we have to wait, but it made me angry inside.

Grupo Niche with "Cali Pachangero, and Una Aventura," Guayacan with "Oiga Mire Vea," Joe Arroyo with "En Barranquilla Me Quedo," and some other Colombian groups were very popular in the late 80's. We hadn't been able to visit our family in Colombia for over 7 years or even been on any vacation in 7 years. I wanted to take the family on vacation to Colombia so we began saving for the trip. August 1988 it took us two years to save enough money but I wanted to go all out and spend like a rich man by taking our family everywhere. We flew to Colombia as a family, no sneaking or fear of any kind. When we landed in Pereira everyone was at the airport waiting for us and as soon as we got out of the plane there was a huge crowd of people cheering, shouting, and waving their arms towards all of us on the plane. It was a great welcoming party at the airport. We could see familiar faces in the crowd and we shouted and waved back to them. There were probably 40 family members at the airport that came to see us. Piedad and I had tears in our eyes from the happiness. Both Paul and Michael were smiling and in culture shock because in the States we only had a few family members but back home there was a giant crowd of cousins shouting their names. They had never felt so popular in their young lives. Those days were wonderful; we shared precious memories with our brothers and sisters and their children. They were all so happy to be with us, especially the children. We went on so many trips with all of them. One of those trips was the river Risaralda that we went to and we had to rent a bus for all of us to go together. The bus driver put on the radio and "Sin Sentimientos" by Grupo Niche was playing. Everyone on the bus began singing the Salsa song together, it was an awesome time. We took the family everywhere and paid for everything, that made me feel so good and I can't explain the feeling but I wanted to be that rich to do that more often. The only reason we were able to do that in Colombia was because the dollar was worth so much more than the peso and we were able to buy much more with our money. Those were the best 4 weeks of our lives, being able to travel so much with the family, eating so well, buying so many things, and making so many others real happy. This time my family didn't reject me, nor make fun of me, nor ignore me; things were different, now they wanted me around them and it felt nice. It was all possible because of money and I wanted more of it. Our vacations came to an end, we flew back to the United States, and it was time to go back to work. We told all our friends of the great time we had and how if it were possible we would want to live in Colombia but with lots of money. It was a farfetched dream but I wanted to make it true. I talked to my brother Juan again and asked him how I could start in the business.

Chapter Five

THE BUSINESS

Son this is when my nightmare began. This is when I decided to walk to close to death, the day I began in the business . . . .

. . . .

In deep rural jungles scattered around Colombia, farmers tend to crops of the coca plant that they must keep hidden from the government. There are workers that cultivate the plant, pick the leaves when they are ready, then take the leaves to the lab. In the lab the chemists get to work and add all the other ingredients to cook and make the cocaine. From there it is dried then taken to an area where many other workers package the cocaine in brick like blocks, then the bricks wait to be shipped to their destinations. From here the drug smugglers pick the packages up and send them to all different locations around the world by many different ways. Some will go to Asia, Europe, Central America, the Caribbean, and the States. This process happens over and over again all over South America. There are so many incredible and unthinkable ways that these drug smugglers come up with to ship the drugs over. The contact that my brother and his friend were working with was a rich young buck that was bored of living a normal rich life and began gambling his money on the cocaine business. I never knew his name and never bothered to ask, since in this business the less you know the longer you live. This young guy lived in the southern part of Colombia and began smuggling cocaine in small amounts into the States, nothing too big so he wouldn't lose too much money if busted. His associates would recruit several people, and then send them here by airplane. Now in these years it was just becoming known to law enforcement so it was not that difficult to bring the merchandise through customs in suitcases. These smugglers were clever though, they would always send a fall guy, one who would get caught by law enforcement so the others would make it across fine. Of course the fall guy never knew that he or she was the fall guy, it was a nasty business. Once across, these people would make contact with the smugglers here in the States and to get paid they would hand over all the merchandise. That's where my brother and his friend came in, they would drive to Miami to pick up the merchandise and bring it to Tampa where they would distribute it to the drug dealers here.

    I told my brother that I was ready to start and he spoke with his boss and as easy as that I was in. My first day came and I met some of Juan's friends. In every job you have co-workers that you make friends with, and Juan had made some friends. I met them, some were nice down to earth people that needed to provide for their families and minimum wage was not cutting it. But there were also those guys that you didn't want them to know where you lived. You know the guys with scary nicknames like Machete, Revolver, Knife, Cannibal, or the ones with dirty nicknames like Gonorrhea, or (Pecueca), meaning foot odor, after all they had those nicknames for some reason, and as odd as it seemed those guys even resembled their nicknames and they were proud of their nicknames too. I was friendly to those guys but never associated myself with them. Instead I only made friends with those guys with normal nicknames such as Feo, Socio, el Negro; the popular nickname was the city that you were from like: Cali, Choco, Buenaventura, or Paisa meaning Medellin, and Rolo meaning Bogota. My job was easy; I would get a bag of it then turn around and take it to someone else. I kept my focus on my business and it was nice seeing all that money coming in, but I was in a spiritual dilemma. I wanted the money but in my heart I knew it was wrong. My conscience would remind me of the consequences all the time, but my life seemed boring to me, I was not happy, and I wanted more. I constantly thought about my Brother Juan's goal and what we had talked about. I seriously wanted to be like the Gringo Rich, who was in fact a rich gringo, back in Miami, but I didn't want my family to find out. What would they think of me? The drug dealer husband, the traqueto father, I couldn't afford them knowing that I was doing this. All these thoughts ran through my head but the money that I was making made all those thoughts disappear. I remembered that if you didn't risk a little in life you didn't get to live a little. After months of mental torment, my fear went away and the money was great. I kept it secret from my family as long as I could. Juan and I talked about investing in Colombia and our ambitious dreams were coming true. The parties got bigger and more frequent and either he or I would have a huge party at our house every Friday or Saturday, and sometimes both Friday and Saturday. We would invite all the new friends we had made since we started the business. The parties would go from 9pm till 7 or 8am the next morning. Our homes were filled with smiles and laughs. Our kids would play and have so much fun while we danced all night to Salsa, Cumbia, and Merengue, and it felt awesome! Juan, Fernando, and I felt like Kings. We felt like Superheroes, but we knew that in the morning we had to be our alter ego; normal waiters and busboys. My job in the restaurant business made it easy to keep it secret. I would finish work at night and I would make my rounds then, and tell Piedad that I was working late or that I went out with some friends. I began saving the money, but I kept it hidden in my closet. I couldn't deposit the money because then the IRS would see it and want their percentage, then wonder how I was making the extra cash. I also kept the merchandise hidden in friends' houses so I would not get caught with it. When I wanted to buy things I had to pay cash, but I kept my spending to a bare minimum also to avoid suspicions.

A few years went by and the 90's rolled in; I was in my 30's and at the age where the music on the radio was not pleasing anymore. Rock and Roll got faster and disturbing, while Rap and Hip Hop was hard for me to understand, and I didn't like Country music too much. I just stuck to my Classic Rock, Latin, and 80's music. Grupo Niche and Guayacan got more popular and Colombian salsa became international. The time came when Juan and Fernando had saved enough money to go to Colombia. We had a farewell party for them and said our goodbyes at the airport. Juan and Fernando told me to be careful and to keep focused on the goal; save enough money to move to Colombia. I didn't want to work minimum wage anymore, I didn't want to wait on tables and live off my tips, and I did not want to work for anyone else but myself. I wanted to be my own boss and make as much as I wanted to with no limits; all of it was coming true. My contacts proposed something to me, they wanted for me to have more responsibility in the business. At first it made me nervous but it had a better earning potential and that called my attention. I had to receive the merchandise, cut it in order to make more, and then distribute it to certain contacts; I also had to drive to Miami or New York City transporting the merchandise to contacts there where they in turn would sell it to their contacts or friends. I picked my clients carefully and I had my way of testing them to see if they were trustworthy. There was an upscale lawyer that was a good client of mine and his friends were his clients, so I supplied them. Another client of mine was a young female accountant with the same deal; I supplied her and her upscale friends also. I did not deal with anybody that fit the drug dealer profile, because either way they were not trustworthy and possibly dangerous or they were undercover cops trying to fit the part.

I heard rumors of the kind of people buying from my friends and other contacts, and you'd think that only certain people bought drugs, but cocaine was so popular that there was no certain profile. You wouldn't believe the clients we had; Celebrities were big into this, the rich upscale people couldn't have enough of it. I also heard of some Doctors, Lawyers, Accountants, Business Owners, and other "Professionals" that were normal clients. It was incredible also knowing who was selling the merchandise; sometimes those who bought it also sold it, and there were lots of business owners here in Tampa selling drugs to keep their businesses growing. Seeing this changed my attitude and I lost respect for people. Piedad and my friends were telling me that I had changed. "Gilberto you look more confident, what is it?" I would just say I didn't know but I did. I began to throw huge parties at my house and pay for everything: the food, the drinks, and the alcohol. I got really confident and it slowly turned into cockiness, because I knew financially, I could quit my job if I wanted to. Unconsciously I was more generous than before. When my wife would ask me where I was getting the extra cash I would yell at her "WORKING HARD" or "LEAVE ME ALONE!" I began to get arrogant and obnoxious. My confidence had improved but I also knew that I had to keep telling lies. I would say things like "Oh yeah, I've been working out" or "I'm doing real well at work." The lies were beginning to stress me out so I decided to start working out, and working harder at my job. My boss even gave me a raise and I became head waiter. All was working well except things at home, Piedad knew something wasn't right and noticed that I carried lots of cash with me. "Gilberto we need to talk." Piedad had said those dreaded words that no man likes to hear come out of their woman's mouth. Of course I answered like every good husband would, "WHAT DO YOU WANT!" Then she replied like every great woman would, "DON'T TALK TO ME LIKE THAT, WHERE ARE YOU GETTING THAT EXTRA MONEY, AND DON'T LIE TO ME!!!" It became a shouting match and we argued all night. "I am not stupid, I see all your new friends and I know the rumors that they all sell drugs! I know your brother and Fernando were doing that and that's how they have houses back in Colombia now!" I denied any involvement in everything but I could not keep my lies up for too long. I eventually caved in and told her the truth. She was so angry and disappointed that she began crying uncontrollably, and she cried all night. She and the kids left that night and slept at her friend's house, and we did not speak for days. I didn't know what to do or how to talk to her again. We eventually did speak and I told her that it was only temporary, but she wanted me to quit. I have always had a way of persuading people and I assured her that it was only for a little while until I saved up enough for property in Colombia. She was not happy with my decision and did not want any part with it, see it, or have our kids find out. I assured her again that it would remain a secret until I was finished. It was done; I kept focus on my business and continued being discrete with my money. I was never stable in my jobs and I didn't like when my bosses yelled at me and everyone argues with their boss sometimes, but now I started yelling back. I was the head waiter for a very nice Italian Restaurant here in Tampa. My boss was working this particular night and some of his pompous rich friends were there dining that evening and I was their waiter. I don't remember exactly why but I had done something wrong and they complained to him. Of course he became upset and called me in the kitchen, so I went. He whispered at me and told me what I had done wrong but he was very demeaning and then he lost his mind when he pinched me in my arm! I began to see red, my blood began to boil; pressure was building in my chest, and in my head! My entire body stiffened and my fists clenched! I lost my mind and began yelling at the top of my lungs! "YOU STUPID S.O.B. EFFING A-HOLE, BLA, BLA, BLA BLA!!! HOW DARE YOU PINCH ME!!! I grabbed him by his throat and raised my right fist and I was going to punch him in his face, but his face was covered in fear with his eyes opened wide, and his arms shielding his face, he begged me to forgive him. "I'm sorry Gilberto, I'm sorry! He was so scared so I didn't hit him, but I pushed him far from me. I began yelling while throwing plates at him and breaking them on the kitchen wall. I quit that night right there. It must have been a real embarrassing situation for him but he never should have touched me. I couldn't believe what he did but I bet he couldn't believe what I did when I threw plates at him. I snapped and did not want anyone else to hurt, humiliate, or embarrass me ever again. He actually called me back, apologized, and didn't want me to quit so I stayed there. Before this attitude change I knew I was angry inside and I blew my top too often and unfortunately my family were the ones who frequently saw that side of me, but now that I was a Resident, and made lots of money, I felt no more psychological restrictions. I had lost my speaking filter and insulted anyone who pissed me off.

    The Florida State Fair was in town and I took my family and friends. We were hungry so I wanted to feed them and we went to the place where all the food was. We could smell the Hamburgers, Cheeseburgers, Pizzas, Hotdogs, Elephant Ears, Deep Fried Doughnuts, and all those other strange foods you see and smell at the fair. We ordered hotdogs and sodas for all of us and when it was time to pay the girl at the register, who was probably right out of high school and spoke with a southern accent, asked me what we had ordered. "Ok we had 8 hotdogs and sodas." I thought I spoke clearly, but she did not understand me and she asked again. "I said 8 hotdogs and 8 sodas." She still did not understand me and said with a sarcastic attitude, "Sorry Sir I do not speak Spanish." This redneck girl just insulted me, I thought angrily and I turned red! Blood boiling again and I blew my top! "SPANISH! SPANISH! I AM SPEAKING ENGLISH YOU STUPID B!@CH, EEFFING THIS, EEFFING THAT! YOU DON'T UNDERSTAND MY ENGLISH, DO YOU UNDERSTAND THIS, EEEFFFF!!!!!!! YYYOOOUUUU!!!!! The girl was shocked and almost in tears but I didn't care. If people thought I was a jerk before, man I was 10 times worse now. My family and friends were so embarrassed that they walked away from the Hotdog kiosk. These crazy outbursts became more frequent and it was normal for me to have them. I felt like "El Patron", The Big Boss, The Head Honcho, and The Incredible Hulk on steroids! I was so hyped up on this life style and I loved it. I was always taking my family and friends out and I would pay for everything cash, I had parties and paid cash, and I even got my nose surgery that I had wanted for years and paid cash. My nose was smaller and more distinguishable, and I thought of changing my name to Bryan again, but that never happened. Cash did not leave a paper trail and if it were possible I would've bought a house or new car in cash, but I just kept on saving for my plan in Colombia.

Cash was building up so fast that I couldn't spend it fast enough and I had nowhere else to hide my money. It was time to start sending it or taking my money down south and begin cleaning it up with businesses. Some of the money I would wire to my brothers and sisters and they were helping me buy property. The other money I was saving here for emergency cases such as medical, car maintenance, or the ever dreaded drug bust/lawyer money. Anyway I just kept up with the plan until I felt I had enough money to leave. Every night after work I would meet up with my friends and go out drinking or go and make some extra money, and I thought life was great. My older son was going to do his Confirmation, the Catholic Ceremony, where I needed to be at on Sunday and Piedad told me on Saturday not to forget and not to go out drinking, but I remember answering in English, "Sure, Sure!" That night I was working and got out at 11pm and my friends and I were going out drinking like usual. I could hear Piedad's voice in my head, "Don't go drinking tonight." I just ignored that and I went to a nightclub with my friends, where we were happy and drinking a lot. I loved music, alcohol, and the social night life; I felt that it kept me young at heart. We partied and danced and drank some more, but it was closing time and we still wanted to keep partying. "Hey guys lets go to an after party club," which stayed open later than most clubs. "Ok let's go" I said ignoring my parental responsibility in the morning. I drove my car and my friend followed in his behind me. It was around 3am and we were driving to the after party club, and I was almost there waiting to make a left turn in the center of the road, yielding to oncoming traffic. The next thing I know is that I wake up laying face up on a hard surface, and I try to open my eyes but I can't see anything because there's some kind of fluid covering my eyes, and my eyes sting. I feel the hard surface and its feels like the road but with little pieces of something I can't make out, now my ears begin to catch noises and make sense of it all. I can hear a siren in the distance, my friend is yelling at me, "GILBERTO, ARE YOU OK? ARE YOU OK?" What is going on, I am thinking, and I hear other voices. "Make room; make room for us to get our equipment in here." I'm still in shock and I try to feel my face to know why I can't see. "Sir, don't move, you just had an accident and you are injured." the voice said. I tried to talk but I had no energy, all I could do was think, what happened? How did I get in an accident, I was driving fine. The paramedics began working on me; they put me on a stretcher, and in the ambulance. I tried to wipe my face and I felt a sharp pain in my shoulder. "Sir, don't move, you had an accident, and you are injured." What? My frustration forced out a question I needed to ask, "What is in my eyes?" The paramedic answered, "Sir, you have glass all over you, and the blood on your face is not letting you see, and it looks like you broke your shoulder. You are very lucky to be alive, you weren't wearing your seatbelt and your shoulder kept you from getting ejected out of your vehicle." His words shocked me and the first thing I thought was, "I can't miss my sons Confirmation." Like if by any chance I would've woken up hung over and gone anyway. The rest was a blur and I began feeling all the pain; my face and my shoulder pain began competing to see which one could hurt me more. The nurses washed my face and got all the glass off of me so I could see. I asked the nurses for pain killers but they told me that my blood/alcohol level was too high for any medicine and I had to sober up first. "What, that's BS!" The pain was excruciating and the time seemed to slow down so that I could feel every second of it. I began to pray for relief, but the pain continued. Piedad got word that I was in an accident and she arrived at the emergency room with a friend. When she walked in the emergency room I heard the nurses ask them, "Are you sure you want to see him?" And they said yes, but when she saw me she began to cry, and her friend ran back outside to vomit. She looked scared and mad at me at the same time and said, "You destroyed your face." I said, "Ah that can be fixed." Everyone who looked at me was disgusted. Finally I had to see what all the commotion was about and I asked for a mirror. The nurses said that it would be better not to look but I insisted. "Ok Mr. Lopez, but I warned you." Filled with intrigue and fear of what I would see, I looked at myself in the mirror and I saw a ghastly face. The glass had cut my face badly and it had cut my eyelids of one of my eyes, leaving the whole eye exposed, like it could fall out if I sneezed. I felt so dumb for what had happened and I wanted my face back. The Doctor said that with some minor surgery, I would look fine and I wanted to believe him, but somehow doubted. I still had pieces of glass in my face protruding from my skin with a little blood. They were going to have to surgically remove all the glass visible to the eyes, but the Doctor said that the body's natural defense would push out the small shards of glass still hidden in my skin. I calmed down and Piedad saw that I was ok because I was talking, and arguing with the nurses to give me pain killers, so she felt at ease now.

As I was thinking that this was so painful and that things couldn't get worse, the Police showed up. "Mr. Lopez, we need to ask you some questions." I got nervous thinking all sorts of things. "What do the Cops want?" But I remembered that I was in a car accident and in the hospital. "What do you guys want, can't you see I'm in pain here!?" I exclaimed with anger and with my Tony Montana Spanish accent. "Mr. Lopez your alcohol level was 0.10 which is well over the legal limit here in the state of Florida. How many drinks did you have before you got in your vehicle and got in this accident?" I knew that they had clever games up their sleeves, and I told them that I didn't have to answer any of their questions. But unfortunately they had all the proof they needed with my blood alcohol level and the obvious car accident so I was technically arrested. I signed their paper and gave them my finger print and I had 10 days to show up in court. I ended up missing my son's confirmation, spending my time in the hospital a few days. My face was a mess with stitches all over looking like Frankenstein and with a broken clavicle being held up by a sling. Ten days later I went to court and got my DUI, my license was suspended and I could not drive. Hahahahaha!!! You think that stopped me from driving, of course not, but I still had to heal though. The accident was pretty serious; when I saw my car I could not believe I was still alive. Back to that night of the accident: As I waited to make a U-turn in my Nissan Sentra Coupe, I was hit by an Isuzu Trooper SUV going 55 mph. It destroyed my car and sent it spinning in circles, while the SUV flipped on its side. I really believe that the driver of the Trooper was also drunk but he was wearing his seatbelt and was still conscious when the Cops arrived, but I was not wearing my seatbelt and was knocked out cold on impact. I was hurled forward when the Trooper hit my car and my body was going to exit through the front windshield but my right shoulder hit the dashboard, keeping me inside the car, breaking my clavicle, and only my face broke through the front windshield. My nose job was recent and luckily it was not ruined in the accident. God kept me alive but gave me some pain to remind me of my consequences. One day I had to go to the supermarket and no one could take me, so I said what the heck, I'll drive myself what could happen. The supermarket was probably two blocks away and when I was coming back I rear ended someone in traffic. "Oh no, why is this happening to me?" I yelled at myself. I went to speak to the person and she was an older lady. She said she was ok, but I knew if the Cops came they would arrest me for driving with a suspended license. I did something I'm not proud of, well many things I'm not proud of. I put the car in reverse and peeled out of there like a flash, then turned the car around and left the scene. Man that was too close, but I decided that I needed to change. I did not want to be the bad guy anymore; I wanted to be a good man, but somewhere different, start over. I decided to quit the drug business and take my family to Colombia.

Chapter Six

HOME SWEET HOME

I remember these days, they were also great ones. It's when I had all that money and we lived in Colombia all together. Do you remember Paul? Yes Dad, I do and they are also great memories for me that I'll treasure forever. Colombia was so beautiful, so dangerous but at the same time so exciting because she was still much uncharted and waiting for us to discover her beauty. I recall those great days . . .

. . . .

We sold all of our furniture and our cars, and any other things that were too big and things that we could buy over there. The rest of our things we packed in boxes and threw them on the plane with us. We were at the airport saying our goodbyes and off we were. I was happy to leave because I knew that I would be my own boss in my legitimate businesses, and I wasn't going to be breaking the law anymore. My wife liked that idea but was a little nervous, and the kids seemed happy but also nervous about this new life ahead of us. The flight was a good one and as soon as the plane landed and touched the Colombian runway, everyone on the plane clapped and cheered knowing that we landed safely and that we were on Colombian soil. The Captain of the plane played a song by Grupo Niche called "Mi Pueblo Natal" and some people's eyes began to water out of happiness to be home. The airport was full of people's families waiting for those getting off the plane including the 50 plus members waiting for us. We had the same welcome back audience as before when we came to visit and it felt great. Our families received us and took us to my mother-in-laws house. Her house was like the family Headquarters because everyone would always get together there and have big parties. We partied all night till the sun rose the next day. In the morning we were woken up by shouting in the street, "Eggs come and get your eggs!" A different voice later shouted, "Tomato, onion, green onion, lettuce, come and get them." We also heard, "THE CHEEEESE!!!" which was the loudest yet.

(All in Spanish of course) One after another the street venders walked through the neighborhoods selling food. Although I was sleepy, I didn't mind the noise of the venders, it was my Colombia singing to me. The morning air was filled with smells of breakfast from many houses: fried eggs, fried steak, arepas (Corn Cake) the Colombia's version of the Tortilla but arepas are thicker, fresh baked bread, and all sorts of baked goods. You could not resist the smell and it would lure you into the kitchen to eat.

We had a house already that I had bought while I was in the States and we soon moved in. I had bought all the furniture and everything we would possibly need before my wife and kids and I arrived. The first few months were very busy, trying to get ourselves organized and the kids registered for school. I had bought a few taxis to bring in money, and I also had two apartments that I rented out so we were pretty much set. We had gone from rags to riches in just a few days; it was like winning the Lotto. I had more money coming in that I knew what to do with so I would spend it with my family on trips and hanging out with my brothers. My businesses were going good and the kids were going to school, and Piedad was a stay at home mom now. It was a great life with no one telling me what to do, no more working for minimum wage, or just living off tips; I was the Boss and I liked it that way. We were living much better now and were treated like the rich. In Colombia, out of respect to a professional or a person with money, anyone attending you calls you Doctor, or Boss, and they treat you very well. It felt silly being called Doctor without having gone to Med School, but I wasn't complaining. I had my children going to good private schools where uniforms were required, and where they would learn the best. I was handling all my businesses and doing Boss things, like giving orders, yelling when things were not done right, firing people, collecting all the money, paying bills, and my favorite part was spending my cash. On the weekends we would go visit my family or Piedad's family, have parties, or go on trips. I loved going to rivers and it became one of our favorite pass times. My brother Juan and I pitched in for the transportation and we'd usually rent a bus for everyone to go, making those the best trips ever. Taking the family out for dinner was fun too. One weekend my wife's family was walking with us in downtown, and we all got hungry. We walked inside a cafeteria style restaurant and had them order whatever they wanted. There were at least 20 of us eating that day, but even then the bill was only around $30 US dollars, which put a big smile on my face. I could get used to this lifestyle, but after living here a few months we noticed that we were used to living the lifestyle from the States, but in Colombia that life was too expensive. We had to tighten up a little and we stopped taking trips so often and especially paying for everyone. Money is an illusion and quickly noticed that the more money I had, the more expensive my problems were. I started focusing on my businesses to increase money flow and spending less money.

Life went on and things began to become routine again. Work then home, then sleep, and repeat it every day. Yawn . . . Stress was building and I was becoming that person that my wife called "Ogre". I needed to relax so I frequently began going out with my brothers Juan and Joel to the nightclubs or to the high end bars where only people with money would go. We would always have a great time. The conversations were about future business ventures or what to spend our money on. On occasion we would take time to remember the times when we were broke and working so hard for so little, and gave thanks that we now had made it big. We were at a really nice nightclub that night on the outskirts of the city, many rich people came here, and just like us, people that were former drug dealers or current drug dealers too. The nightclub had a rustic look to it. There were certain booths that were only for V.I.P. and had curtains that concealed what was inside. The lights were dimmed just like every nightclub, and music was playing. As we were talking, I saw a man come in dressed in dark clothing sporting a black leather trench coat and he had an angry look on his face. He asked one of the employees something and he pointed the man to one of the booths at the other end of the club, and the man continued. I didn't think anything different and kept talking with my brothers. A few minutes later we heard the loud sounds. BANG, BANG, BANG!!! AAAHHHHH!!!! Gunshots followed by women screaming; we all knew exactly what those sound were. "What is going on in here?" Everyone ducked under their tables, and my brothers Juan and Joel pulled out their guns, I did not have one. We then saw that same man come out from one of the booths carrying a man on his shoulder. He quickly walked out of the club with other men following him. As they walked pass us I took a quick look at the man hung over the other man's shoulder without them seeing me and I noticed that the guy was dead! He had been shot and was bleeding from his head as they walked away with him leaving a messy blood trail. They left the club in a hurry taking the body with them. I was expecting for the manager to call the Police or for them to be in shock, but the employees' quickly grabbed mops and rags, cleaned up the bloody trail and the mess they left at the table and went back to business like nothing had happened. My jaw dropped to the floor, nothing had been done, a man was murdered and no one cared. Some customers did grab their things and left in a haste and that's what we did. From then on I was more careful where I went. Colombia was definitely more exciting and dangerous but this was home now.

We knew that things would be different here but as the months went by we noticed that things in Colombia were very, very different than the United States. We were now living in Colombia in the 90's and the drug war between the Cartels was very fresh. If we thought Miami in the 80's was bad, well that was nothing compared to this. Pablo Escobar was killing lots of innocent people; car bombs were his signature trademark along with putting hits on Police Officers and Government workers. There were more bodies dropping like flies left and right, more than anybody cared to have. He even had someone put a bomb in a busy pharmacy in the city where we were living in and it killed many innocent people. Hitmen known as Sicarios were very busy assassinating their boss's competition and anyone who defied their power. It was The Wild West; the way of the gun in Colombia meaning: the power was in those carrying the gun. Unlike in the States that if anyone got murdered or just died out in the public, the Police were discreet enough to cover the body with a blanket and have barricade tape that kept everyone far away from the body. But here if someone dropped dead or was killed, there was no blanket and the barricade tape was very close to the body. So anyone and everyone walked up to the tape and could get a good glimpse of the corpse. The country was corrupt and killing had become a normal day thing. Of course it was still terrifying though to those who had to witness people getting shot and murdered in the streets. There were jokes that said, "Here people don't just die, they are made dead." Or neighborhoods that had signs that read, "Here many are born, but few are raised." Why all this dark humor, because it was a harsh reality. The News was covered with everyday murders and scenes of bloody, shot up corpses. My kids had never seen a dead body until we lived here so we kept them aware of all the dangers and told them never to be alone in the streets. I could not believe some of the things we heard of, although in the small city where we were living in was much calmer than the other big cities and their drug wars. Homeless people and homeless kids were dangerous because they were known to rob people too. Thieves were also prominent and dangerous, and we began to experience their trickeries. One afternoon that I wasn't home, some unknown men came to the house in a truck and asked for me. Piedad knew better than to open the door and she spoke to them from the second floor balcony. These unknown men said, "Hi Mrs. Lopez, we are some friends of your husband and Gilberto told us to wait for him inside since he is on my way." Piedad was smarter and answered, "Yes that's right he is on his way, just wait for him right there." The men looked nervous and left not even waiting for a minute. Different thieves tried similar tricks frequently. These were all ploys to get inside and rob us. They knew all sorts of details about us that were pretty scary and made us wonder who the heck was giving them that kind of personal information. Thank God that Piedad never let them in.

My mother had a stroke and was in serious condition in the hospital. All my family got together and we knew it was time to be ready for the worst. The Doctor told us that my mother would not walk or talk anymore. She was bedridden and would need 24 hour nursing from now on. We all were crushed by the news and cried. My mother did not know who we were anymore. Sometimes she would smile at my brother but no one else. It brought up many scars I had from my childhood and how I felt that she didn't love me and rejected me by calling me "that man" and not by my name. It hurt and now my hopes of her apologizing to me or telling me she loved me were gone. My brother Juan took the responsibility to care for her until she passed away.

My wife and I began having drama again, because I was going out too much and coming home drunk. She worried that one night I would not come home because of getting in an accident, or getting shot and killed by someone. My brothers and I loved to party and that's all we did, and my wife knew that in those parties there were always beautiful young women looking to steal rich men away from their wives. Those women were always around the party scene in the States, but in the States they didn't flirt with me much, but here they were very intense, and she had good reason to be nervous about that. Arguing with Piedad was getting worse and my oldest son was having problems in school. He was a good student in the States but education in Colombia is much harder and he was failing in school and that made him miserable. Nothing that I would tell my family seemed to make things better and I was not exactly a model husband or father. I didn't know what to do, and only after 7 months I was beginning to get tired of Colombia. We hid the fact that I had been a (Traqueto) Drug Dealer in the United States but people in the neighborhood were so nosy always asking all sorts of prying questions, who we were, what we did in the States, how much we earned, what University we attended. They suspected what I had done and got a kick out of asking personal questions. We knew exactly what they were trying to do. The snobs here were just as bad as those in the United States, they wanted us to know that they had earned their money and had attended Universities, and had careers, unlike us. They were going to think whatever they wanted to about us, and I got tired of their prying questions so I began answering, "That's none of your damn business!" I got tired of many things especially the violence and the insecurity. The Police were not much help; since the corruption was so bad you had to worry about them too. You always needed to watch over your shoulder to see if you were being followed by anybody and the danger of the drug wars made you wonder if the car nearest you would explode. Paying your bills was torture having to wait long lines for hours just to make a payment. All these annoying things and the problems at home were making me wonder why we moved down here. It wasn't till one incident to close to home made me decide.

My sons were at their grandmother's house where all the cousins would meet and play soccer, while Piedad and I were out doing errands. There was a young man that had been hanging around the neighborhood that nobody recognized, he seemed worried, concerned about something. My kids and their cousins had seen the young man several times that day, but thought nothing about it. All the kids that lived on that block were outside playing including my kids. One block down from their grandmother's house was a real nice house of three floors that had an awesome Toyota SUV and German Shepherds guarding the house. Later that day the owner of the house got inside his Toyota SUV with his wife and backed out of their garage. As the SUV entered our street a motorcycle with two young men pulled up behind it. The motorcycle revved up its engine to pass the SUV but instead of passing it, the two young men rode their bike right beside the SUV. BANG, BANG, BANG, BANG!!! Muzzle flashes and small explosions! Machine gun fire with the sound of the casings hitting the floor, accompanied by the screams of young children and their mothers! AAHHHH!!! The two men were Sicarios and the one bike rider was shooting at the SUV driver in the head with an Uzi! The SUV crashed on the sidewalk in someone's garden as the two men got off their bike to assure the man was dead and shot him again. They jumped on their motorcycle and followed by another truck they sped off peeling out of the block. Everyone on the block was searching for their children to make sure they were all alright. Miraculously none of the people on the block were hurt, but the dead man's wife was screaming for help. She fell out of the SUV bleeding from her legs because she had been shot several times as well. Two young men from the block, one was Piedad's nephew, waved down a taxi, pulled the dead man out and jumped inside the taxi with him and the lady and rushed to the nearest hospital. When we heard what had happened I was upset because both of my kids were in the neighborhood. Thank God my oldest was not there and my youngest was inside a friend's house, but some of my wife's nieces and nephews saw the entire thing. That was enough of the violence and I didn't want my family living in the middle of this. I spoke to my wife and told her that we were moving back to the US. When the kids heard they were very happy, and we began selling our things again. I flew back to Tampa first and began getting everything ready for my family. We had lived in Colombia for only 8 months, and sure we were going to miss the family and the unforgettable times we had together, but my kids were not used to Colombia and they loved the United States.

Back in Tampa, the year was 1992 and my kids were back in school. I found work as a waiter again since I had been doing it so long and had friends in the restaurant business. Piedad got her old job back and it was like we had never left. We were going on trips with our friends and having parties at our house again. Tampa was a small city and it wasn't long before I bumped in to old friends. They quickly offered me my old job back, and I didn't disagree; extra money was always tempting, so I began in the business again. We lived a little more modest now and I didn't spend money like before, but my wife still didn't like my extracurricular activities. Soon after my brother Joel, the one who needed me to come through the Bahamas with his family, came to the States to work; he was a Legal Resident. He had divorced his wife years before but they were still friends and their daughter lived with her. He was staying with us in Tampa and he began working in some office. A few months went by when he received a call from Colombia with horrible news. His daughter was frantic on the phone and crying, she told him that her mother had been murdered. Joel began crying but we didn't know what to do, there are no words that can help in a situation like this. My brother packed his bags and left the following day. He later told us what happened. She had lent money to some friends of her current boyfriend long before but they did not want to pay her back. She threatened them with going to the Police or suing them to get her money back. These men were (Traquetos) drug smugglers in Colombia, meaning that they could be very evil people. She was eating lunch one afternoon at an outdoor Café, when some man (a Sicario) came up to her and shot her dead. The Traquetos had put a hit on her to avoid paying her and preventing her from suing them. They were never charged because they were very powerful and evil men. We were all very hurt from the loss, because she was a friend of all of us. She was a very talented artist who created beautiful paintings. We had bought one many years ago and till this day it is still in the family hanging in a living room. Joel stayed in Colombia to take care of their daughter.

Tampa was a little bigger now and I was trying to behave. It was the same old routine again, go to work, come home, sleep, and repeat the next day. It drove me crazy, I had to go out drinking, and I had to hang out with friends. After work I would go out with my friends but didn't drink like I did before to avoid any more DUI's. I was constantly going out at night and when you're surrounded by bad influences you tend to make bad decisions. There was a very attractive woman that began to show her interest in me and I began to have an affair. My wife found out and she was devastated, Piedad cried every night and blamed my lifestyle as a drug dealer. I was crazy about that woman for some reason; I would look for her like an addiction. Piedad hated me and the arguments at home were horrible so I began spending less time at home and I was always out. I didn't care who I hurt as long as I was happy and I kept seeing the other woman. I was contemplating leaving my wife, but I felt guilty leaving my kids. My relationship with this woman was wonderful, but soon after when all the lust was consumed I discovered that I had opened Pandora's Box. This woman had become so jealous that I was still with Piedad that she began calling my house and insulting my wife. She started showing up at my job just to argue with me. "Why are you still with your wife, don't you love me?!" "Yes I love you!" I would answer her but inside I knew that I didn't. This woman was crazy, and then she began spreading rumors saying that she was pregnant with my kid and that I would beat her with my gun! I didn't even own a gun, and the whole pregnant thing was her sick way of trying to manipulate me. Rumor after rumor she spread about us and how I was a bastard for having an affair, getting her pregnant and refusing to leave my wife for her. When she began keying my car and scratching insults in the paint, I had had enough of her. Man did I feel dumb, Piedad never made a scene like that, or start rumors about me, or scratch my car, nothing, she was a saint. We were just roommates now living together to keep our kids happy and thinking that we would never divorce, but the damage was done and it was my fault. I ended the affair with the psycho woman and prayed that I wouldn't find a dead rabbit in my soup or get killed by that nut. I asked my wife to forgive me but she said. "Gilberto you have done the worst thing you can do to anybody, betrayal. I will never trust you again and I don't know if I could forgive you." Her words were hurtful but what was more hurtful was my guilt because she did not leave me nor did she give me too much grief.

We tried to put the past in the past and I tried to live a normal life, but I remembered that normal people don't sell cocaine. I worked and occasionally went out with my friends and one night my shift had ended early so I went to the local bar where some friends showed up. I was in to my second beer when an old friend of the business came in and said hello. "Gilberto, how are you man?" It was El Negro that was his nick name. "I'm good Negro, and you?" We were talking for a while and he asked me if I could give him a ride home. "Yeah, sure thing man, no problem." I drove him to his house and at his house there was a party. "Gilberto come in and have some dinks man." I didn't want to stay and told him I'd have just one beer and leave. "Ok make yourself at home." I knew his family and some other people there so I sat down to have my beer. I think I was there for 10 minutes talking, listening to music when, POP, POP, POP, POP!! We heard gunshots coming from inside the house! Most of the guests started running for the door, which I should've been doing also, and of course women were screaming. But the family that lived there ran inside to see who was shooting a gun in their house, and my dumb ass also went. The shooting was coming from inside the bathroom and when we looked inside we saw some short 5'ft 4" thug shooting at a 6'ft black man inside the tub! The man in the tub was El Negro; he had fallen inside the tub and was trying to kick the gun out of the thug's hand, while the thug dodged kicks to his face and arms and continued shooting at El Negro! "LEAVE HIM ALONE!!!" I don't know what came over me but I was furious and I ran at the gunman and tackled him, but the gunman was younger and stronger and he was able to push me off of him. I had Negro's family behind me yelling at the guy, but he had a gun and turned it on us! The thug began shooting at us and we all scattered like roaches trying to get out of the house! The thug gave chase as he shot at us and he decided to go after me! I ran to my car when the thug caught up to me and tripped me! When I fell he kicked me in the face which flipped me over on my back, and I was looking up at him! Time seemed to slow down like in super slow motion! He pointed his gun at me and fired several shots! My eyes focused on the gun's barrel as it looked at me and puffed smoke from its mouth followed by the deafening sound of gunfire. I prayed and asked God not to let me die, and at that very second the man ran out of bullets and ran away! My heart was beating so hard, I was dizzy, and had tunnel vision! Quickly I got in my car but then I noticed that I was bleeding from my stomach! I WAS SHOT SEVERAL TIMES!!! Instead of driving to the hospital, I drove home to get Piedad. I did not want to go to the hospital alone for some reason; I guess if I was going to die, I didn't want to die alone. When she saw me she was worried and kept asking me what had happened. "Let's go, let's go I have no time to explain!" We arrived at the emergency room and when they saw me, they quickly took me in yelling at one another, "Shot victim!" I had never seen nurses move so fast to attend to me. My shirt was cut away exposing the bullet wounds, they were stopping the bleeding, and the nurses began looking for exit wounds and if the bullets were still inside of me. All the shots were on my right side, and they counted the holes. "It appears he has three entrance wounds, but only two exit wounds!" "Find the bullet!" the nurses exclaimed, and shortly after one said, "I found it I found it!" I'm thinking, wow they are good! But it was very noticeable; the third bullet had rested on my stomach near the surface of my skin pushing my skin up and I could actually feel it inside. The nurses said that I was lucky to be alive but I knew that luck had nothing to do with me being alive. God had saved me again from death. Usually Doctors tell you that cholesterol is bad and being fat is bad too, but this time the Doctor said that my fat had saved me from the bullets. That was good news for me because I loved to eat. Apparently the bullet caliber was of a 380 pistol. Two bullets hit my fat, missed my organs, and exited immediately, and the third one hit my love handle and my fat slowed it down. It was serious but comical at the same time and my friends that visited me in the hospital made jokes.

    The good news was that I was still alive but the bad news was that the Police were at me again with their questions. "Mr. Lopez why were you there? Mr. Lopez did you know that this shooting was drug related? Mr. Lopez did you know that your friend that got shot is a known drug dealer? Mr. Lopez, are you a drug dealer?" They just kept asking me all these questions and I kept denying everything. "I'm not answering anymore questions." They had no evidence to arrest me so I denied any involvement. While in the hospital, I heard from my friends that El Negro almost died. He was shot eleven times, in the legs, in the arms, and in his abdomen wounding his liver. The Doctors removed all the bullets from his body and had to remove a part of his liver, and he was in critical condition. I was glad that he survived but now the Cops were coming around my house often asking more questions about that night, but I knew it was more of an excuse for them to investigate me. "Mr. Lopez what do you do? How can you afford your lifestyle on a waiter's salary?" All I could do was just ignore them but I knew it was a matter of time before they found out the truth. I got so nervous that I decided to leave to Colombia again and let things die down. I moved my family back with me as soon as I could, but this time my oldest son Paul did not come with us and decided to stay and finish High School. That was very hard on Piedad, she felt so bad and said that we had abandoned our son, but I assured her that we would have him visit us twice a year.

It was the fall of 1993 and we were living in Colombia again just a year and a half after we had moved back to the States. "Wow Gilberto you're going to give your family whiplash from all the quick moving from here to there and back." "When are you going to make up your mind Gilberto?" These were some of the jokes people kept telling me because of my unstableness. I just thought "Whatever I prefer this better than getting arrested and going to jail." I had bought taxis again and I still had my apartments that brought in money monthly so I was living like the rich again. Life went on; Michael was doing fine in school and Piedad was doing fine at home too, but not having Paul around and not knowing what he was doing or if people were treating him well was tough. The country had not changed much since we were living there last. Colombia has been in a civil war with rebel groups since 1948 or so. These rebel groups are huge in numbers, very well equipped, and organized. They had all the same weapons as the military that they bought from the Communist groups like Cuba for example. There were three main rebel groups: The FARC, Revolutionary Forces of Colombia; The ELN, Liberating National Army; and the AUC, Auto Defenses of Colombia. There are others but these are the biggest and oldest. They make their living by growing the drugs for the Cartels, acting as their personal Armies, and kidnapping wealthy civilians for ransom, and even known to recruit their armies by kidnapping young children. They were very scary and very real in the country. They also would go into small towns and take whatever they wanted and killed anybody who opposed them. I was working in transporting goods to other cities and I needed to drive some goods to the capital. Bogota was about 10 hours away up and down huge mountains surrounded by large dense jungle. I drove a Chevy pickup truck and asked my friend to help me drive those long hours through the curvy nightmare; people were known to get motion sickness riding on a bus to Bogota. The road was famous for its sickening twists and turns and deadly drops into the deep jungle. We drove there and reached our destination in the capital with no problem and the motion sickness almost got my friend. On our way back as we were driving it began to rain, the night's darkness reached us at 6pm and the rain continued softly. The night was pitch-black darkness and the moonlight was behind some giant mountain because I couldn't see her light. All we could see were our headlights lighting the road just a few feet ahead of us making it a very slow drive. "Look what is that?!" I slammed on the breaks because there was a man standing in the road. My friend and I looked pale like if we had seen a ghost. The man was wearing a camouflage uniform with a green raincoat and his machine gun hanging from a sling around his torso. We thought "ok it's the military", but then remembered that the Rebels wore the same uniforms but were recognizable by a bandana around their arm and the Rebels also wore rubber rain boots. Around this man's right arm he wore his bandana and he was sporting his rubber boots too. We thought the worst, "we're dead, he's going to shoot us dead and take my truck." He walked up to my window and I rolled it down so he could say what he was going to say. The Rebel Soldier said, "Good evening gents." We answered politely avoiding pissing him off. Then he said, "I am a Soldier with the ELN and me and my comrades need a ride. Can you gents help us out?" What else were we going to say? I liked being alive and didn't want to die covered with bullet holes in some dark Colombian jungle. "Sure we can help just say what you need." All we had seen was him but he waved his men out from the wet jungle and 4 more Rebel Soldiers came out. He got in the front with us and the others jumped in the back of the truck. "Just drive and I'll tell you where to stop." "Ok" I said to him keeping conversation to a minimum. We drove and everything looked the same, dark and wet, but the Rebel Soldier knew exactly where he was at and a few hours later told me to stop. "Thank you gents for your service and in helping the cause have a goodnight." He said as they got off my truck and ran into the jungle with his men. My friend and I drove away slowly, we were pale white in the face, and didn't say a word for hours, and just knowing that we were still alive was overwhelming.

My mother was still sick and suffering a lot. I went to visit her and when she saw me she smiled. My mother had never done that to me and immediately my eyes watered. I got closer to her and she held and squeezed my hand which caused me to cry like a child. I felt that my mother was apologizing to me and telling me she loved me. I would never forget that day. Months after that day my mother passed away after 2 years of being bedridden from her stroke. All my brothers and sisters made it to the funeral and we all said goodbye.

Colombia was beautiful but for some reason the USA called us again. We lasted 10 months this time and again saw ourselves moving back to Tampa in the summer of 1994. We adjusted and bought a house in Town-N-Country on the west side of the County. Paul moved back in with us and we were a family again. I felt then that Tampa had become my home sweet home and I didn't want to leave her anymore. Piedad got her old job back but as for me I decided to buy a tow truck and start my own business instead of working in restaurants again. But I had no idea how to work the truck and had some very embarrassing moments. I sold the truck shortly after because of my lack of experience with a tow truck. A friend told me to become his business partner and help him manage a Latin restaurant, but I declined thinking of the awful mess and stress of having a restaurant. Piedad told me that I had spoiled myself rotten selling cocaine because I didn't want to work in anything else, I just ignored the comments and kept going. Now that we were back in Tampa our friends joked again with me saying "Hey Gilberto we want you guys to give us back the going away gifts and the welcome back gifts because you leave then come back and do it again and again. Ha ha ha!!!" They were right and I didn't even want to think of all the money I was spending moving back and forth, it was ridiculous. I was avoiding the same old habits that had gotten me in trouble before but always seemed to end up selling drugs again. I kept telling myself just a little more, just a little more. I really was spoiled, I didn't want to work for anyone else, and the easy money made it really difficult to quit selling drugs. One day my son came up to me and told me that he saw a helicopter fly really close over our house. That he and his friend looked up and saw a man in a suit wearing sunglasses looking down at them. They thought it was strange but I knew that it was the Cops snooping around. I also got home late one night from drinking and was drunk, I noticed an unmarked squad car driving by my house. I quietly hid in my front yard to see what they were up to. The car parked across from my house and began shinning its high beams at my house. I guess they were trying to see if there was any drug activity there at night. Now being drunk and impulsive I wasn't thinking and I came out from where I was hiding and I began yelling all sorts of insults at the Cop, but when he saw me he drove away quickly. Piedad heard me cursing outside and came out to bring me inside. Those bastards were investigating me but I was on to them and I wasn't going to get caught with my merchandise, I also had become too proud. With all that was going on in my life this made the stress worse.

Although I was still selling cocaine I only sold in small portions because of the hard punishments. I also kept my stash of coke in a friend's house to avoid getting caught with it, but I began noticing that the cocaine was being tampered with. My friend's girlfriend was a coke head and loved powdering her nose and I knew she was sticking her darn nails in it taking free hits off my stuff. DARN B!@CH. I had to take it out of there and hide it in my house but it was only temporary until I found somewhere else to hide it. With the cops having me under a microscope I was starting to feel the pressure build but I was cocky and it had become a challenge for me. I didn't know what the big deal was with drugs. To me it was just a product that I sold to customers. My philosophy was that Colombia produced

Coffee which was the world's pep in the morning and produced Cocaine which was the world's pep at night. Colombia also produced great entrepreneurs and this is how I felt about myself. I was only a business man with a great product that was in great demand, that's how I justified myself. I also felt that the government didn't want too many people making lots of money and by controlling small businesses with big taxes proved that they always wanted to control us and I hated that. Out of curiosity I tried some cocaine and marijuana but I didn't see the big deal. The biggest rule we followed was never to use your own product or you've probably heard the saying, "never get high off your own supply", and I never wanted to be addicted to anything.

Everything was normal, and I did my job and brought home the bacon. The cops stopped spying on me or so I thought they did anyway. Another one of my wife's sisters was coming to the States and we had to pick her up in Miami. While we were down in Miami I bumped into my cousin Antonio, the old school Miami Vice drug dealer stuck in the 80's. He had been arrested once already and paid his sentence. He had been so rich in the 80's and after he went to prison he lost everything, his wife left him, and his son never wanted to talk to him again because of the way he had treated them. I felt bad for him but he seemed ok. Antonio didn't know how to do anything else but sell cocaine so that's what he was still doing. When we met that day he told me about what he was doing. "Gilberto, I'm working on a great deal that is going to make me lots of money. Do you want in?" He asked me and I couldn't refuse when he told me how much. "Ok let's do it cousin." He grabbed his gym bag full with a giant stash of cocaine, and he followed me to Tampa. I began making lots of calls to my friends trying to see who was interested in buying it or helping me sell it. My business contacts were trying to tell me something but they seemed reluctant on the phone. "Gilberto we need to talk in person man." I met with my friend the Lawyer guy, "Gilberto we've been noticing strange people asking questions about our business, and that new contact that we have, you know that coked out woman, well she makes me nervous man. She might be an informant for the Cops. I just want to let you know and I'm not doing any business with her." I was so anxious to sell what Antonio had brought that I wasn't really scared about what he said. "Are you sure that you guys are not just exaggerating? She's just some coke head woman, and all coke heads look nervous and scared." He said, "Ok man, don't tell me that I didn't warn you." That meeting was not what I wanted to hear, I wanted to hear, "sure thing man we'll help you sell it and we'll make this much profit from that!" I thought, "Whatever let me talk to some other contacts that I have then." I was calling everyone to see who could help me and I got caught up with work that I was not thinking straight. A week had passed and I wasn't having much luck. My beeper went off so I called the number back. "Hello is this Gilberto?" It was the coke head woman. "Yes it's me, how can I help you?" She wanted a hit, and asked if she could buy a small amount. "Ok let's meet at this little plaza off Hanley Rd." She agreed so I grabbed what she wanted and drove to the plaza. I parked my car and I saw her from a distance, but as soon as I stepped out from my car I began to hear men yelling. "Sheriff's Office! Sheriff's Office! Put your hands up! Before I could do anything I was tackled to the floor. "Put your hands behind your back, you are under arrest for the possession and illegal distribution of cocaine!" My heart sank to the bottom; I could not believe what was happening. I was cuffed and put in the back of a Police vehicle. I wanted to hide my face from the world from my embarrassment. As I was being arrested, the Sheriff's Office Narcotics team was at my house knocking at the door. Piedad and my youngest son were home when they answered the door to about twenty cops. She was greeted by a Spanish speaking cop who asked if they could search the house. We didn't know our rights and she let them in without a search warrant. They quickly found Antonio's gym bag with all that crap from Miami, and lots of money I had hiding in the house. They also searched my car and found what I was going to sell to the Narc, Informant coke head woman. All I could think was "Sapa" a Colombian slang word we use for informants meaning Toad, similar to the word "Rat" used by the Italians. That Sapa sold me out and now I was under arrest. I was charged with illegal possession with the intent to sell of a controlled substance, and I was booked at the Orient Road Jail.

That night I was processed, got my mug shots taken, and stripped searched then forced to wear the orange jump suit with the inmate number on the back. My face was all over the News, and Piedad began getting the phone calls from friends and acquaintances asking if it was true. Unfortunately for me this nightmare was true. I was filled with pride and denial and refused to believe that I was a criminal, "I am not a criminal." I would say to them, and they would respond to me, "Sure you're not we are just harassing you that's all." They mocked me and laughed at me, it was better just to keep silent. Piedad and my kids began visiting me but I was so angry and I blamed everyone else for my situation. I gave Piedad instructions on what to do in regards to a Lawyer and what to do with my money. I had faith that this was all just a big mistake and that as soon as I went to trial that I would be a free man. Besides I only sold small amounts; that was not a big deal,

PAUL A. LOPEZ

but more of a nuisance to the cops, right? I told myself that everything was going to be alright, I'll be set free soon, and I'm not a criminal. Night after night having to sleep so close to all these unknown criminals infuriated me. I hated everyone around me, I was nothing like them. I was only a business man providing for my family that had been wronged by the judicial system; this was all a mistake. I'll be a free man soon.

Chapter Seven

LOCKED UP

Lights switching on and the Corrections Officers yelling "wake up, wake up!" were the first things I heard every morning. "Get up now, let's go now, move, move!" We were woken up and taken to eat breakfast, then were made to clean up certain areas and throw the trash away. We had daily chores and were given free time in the afternoons. We were herded everywhere together like cattle and the Corrections Officers were the Cowboys rounding us up and taking us to breakfast, lunch, and dinner, then the ever so frightening showers, and finally to our cell blocks where our doors were locked up for the night. Some nights I would quietly cry myself to sleep pressing my face into my pillow to muffle the sound. I could hear others crying quietly in their beds also. In the day everyone was a hard ass incapable of feeling fear or crying but at night you could hear the true feelings come out and turn into quiet sobs disguised with coughs and throats clearing. This went on for weeks until I had my arraignment in court.

  I was given a trial date and my bond was set at $100, 000. My brother Silvio bonded me out and put his house on lean, so if I ran the Bail Bonds would keep his house. I had made bond and was let go until my trial but with conditions of course. It felt so good to be free and I never wanted to go back to Jail again. My brother and I spoke about me leaving the country and he losing his house but he was fine with that. My wife was angry at me, "How could you leave and have your brother's house taken away! This is your mess and you're going to run like an irresponsible little boy." I did not like what she was saying but it was the truth and it bothered me that I was acting like a coward. That didn't matter, it was me facing time in prison not her so I left to Colombia soon after my bond. Everyone in my family was so angry with me for leaving that I was not welcomed anywhere. I didn't know what to do. I asked Piedad to come to Colombia with the children but she refused to follow me anymore. I was so angry at everyone, how could they betray me like that. I didn't understand why they wanted me to go to prison. My wife didn't want to be with me anymore, she told me to be a man and face my punishment. I was so scared and I felt like a lost child. I was approaching my time to appear in court again and if I didn't show, I would become a fugitive, my brother's house would be taken away from him, and I would lose my family. I was trapped between a rock and a hard place, and there was no winning for me; I would lose either way. How could God have let this happen to me, why did I get caught?! With no other solution in mind, I decided to come back to the States and face the consequences.

    My trial began in the spring of 1995; I was taken into custody again where I was stripped of all my belongings and given the orange jumpsuit. I pled not guilty and I began spending my money on lawyers to try to keep me free. It didn't matter to the Prosecutors that I had a family; they were throwing the book at me as hard as they could. As the months went by I saw many undercover cops take the stand for the State and claim that they had purchased drugs from me in large amounts. It was all an attempt from them to give me hard time in prison, but it was not true. They took the stand claiming that I was a big fish and that I was selling large amounts of cocaine for years now. It disgusted me how they could lie about me like that, but my lawyer assured me that those were their tactics to scare me into a plea bargain. Sure enough, they would meet with me between court dates and tell me that I was facing a long time in prison and that I should give people's names to lighten my sentence. I refused to be a "Sapo" a dirty rat, which was the lowest you could be in this business. Everyone knew that Sapos would die sooner or later along with their Sapo family. In Colombia there was a saying (sapos mueren estripados) meaning "Toads die squashed." I could not give anyone away, because I would be the worst of the worst, and that would put me and my family at risk of getting killed. The Prosecutors kept on with their barrage of witnesses and trying to convince the judge and jury that I was the most evil man alive; heck I was also convinced that I was worse than Pablo, but I was a nobody in the drug business that was the embarrassing truth. It didn't matter what the truth was, people hated drug dealers, big or small, and the Judge hated them even more because her brother had been a serious drug addict and died of an overdose. She had a personal vendetta against drugs and drug dealers, without a doubt that was probably her sole motivation in becoming a judge, to seek revenge on my kind. My trial lasted about 5 months and it was about time for sentencing. The day came and I was so scared that I couldn't feel my legs, my stomach turned and twisted with anxiety, and I had the cold sweats. The Judge had me speak and my voice cracked while I tried to apologize for my mistake. "I'm, I'm sorry for what I've done. I know that I have broken the laws of this country and I'm very sorry."

My family and closest friends looked at me with watered eyes. The Judge spoke and told the people of the court what she thought of me and people like me. "Mr. Lopez I have seen many people in my court room for the same offense, and they all apologize just like you, and I have given lighter sentences thinking they have learned from their mistake. But then they go back to the same thing when freed. So frankly I don't believe you or anyone else that stands where you're standing anymore. Therefore it is my responsibility to do my job correctly, and I do hereby sentence you to no less than 15 years in a maximum security prison and it begins now! Bailiff, take him away." The sound of her gavel slamming made me nauseas, my family and I were in shock and all of us began to cry. "That's not possible, I'm sorry, I'm sorry, please don't do this to me." My family came to say goodbye to me as they took me away in shackles. I couldn't stop crying, but I was also filled with anger with the State and the Judge, this was not justice.

The moments after were a blur and I only remember getting put on a bus and sent to processing to get shipped away to a maximum security prison. The minutes of the days were torment, 15 years to go meaning I would get out in 2010. How was prison going to be? I immediately thought of the 80's movie, Midnight Express, and me ending up crazy. I was sent to some prison far north from Tampa in the middle of nowhere. I reached that place and it was hell. Everyone's head was shaved bald, and given new orange pajamas, and we were all maggots, according to all the Corrections Officers. They were like Drill Sergeants, I had never served in the military but I heard inmates that had saying that it was like the military. We were not allowed to speak to anyone; we had to form lines everywhere we went, and could not look around. If we did we were pulled aside and yelled at in our faces and punished some way or another. I thought that jail was tough but prison was unbearable. I was nervous about all the things you hear about prison, about pissing off the wrong guy and getting stabbed, or getting raped by some sick bastard. All these things were a new hell for me but I had to keep a hard shell. I didn't show my fear to anyone in prison or else you would become someone's prison girlfriend. I kept quiet and to myself, but thankfully I was able to make some friends. In prison you tend to keep with your race and I kept with all the Latinos, Whites with Whites, and Colored with Colored. The Cubans in our group were deadly and had no problem in killing anyone, so I associated myself with them for protection. Although I was where I was, I still prayed to God for protection and luckily the Cubans and Latinos were cool with me. I also was thankful that I had lost my sex appeal because nobody tried to bother me sexually. But unfortunately for some, like the young kids in prison, that was a horror of everyday life. I was bald and not having any sunlight for a while I looked white so I had to speak in Spanish to get recognized as a Latino. The Colored and the Whites hated each other and were always messing with one another. I was mistaken for a white guy one day and I had some colored guy skip me in line. I asked him what his damn problem was but he just looked at me and told me, "What the hell you gonna do white boy?!" I had to make my presence known and I began cursing at him in Spanish, "Negro HP!" I kept cursing at him and pushed him telling him. "Do you know who I am you black piece of sh!!! I'm Colombian motherf!!!! You better respect me before you're dead!!!" He saw that I was Latino and backed off. "Oh, you a Papi? My bad papi, don't mean no disrespect man, I thought you were a white boy." I am not racist whatsoever, but in here you had to talk the talk and walk the walk or else you'd be in trouble. In this prison the Cubans ran the show and no one liked messing with the Latin crew. Thankfully he backed off and left me alone, but I quickly knew that I needed to grow my hair and get a tan.

Visiting day was here and I got to see my family, Piedad and the kids looked sad, but that's how things were and I couldn't do anything about it. They had driven 5 hours to come and see me and could only stay for an hour, it was upsetting. In prison I learned quickly who my true friends were, out of all my supposed friends that came to all my parties and went on trips with us, only two friends would visit me in prison. Piedad even had two bastards try to hit on her while I was in here and she had to tell them never to come or call again. I had lost all my friends and never wanted to see those people again. There were so many things out of my control, unexplainable things. We owned property in Colombia and it would have been enough money coming in a month to help my wife. But on the same day that I had been arrested there had been a massive earthquake in Colombia that severely damaged one of those apartments, the people moved out, and I could not sell it damaged. I sold the house to pay for my lawyer and now there wasn't enough to help my wife. She was going to have to get another job to help cover the bills. There was only some money saved and I told her to use it in case of an emergency. I felt that all I had worked so hard for was all crumbling down around me. In prison I learned to spend my time wisely, I began working, taking a class, and I began reading a lot. I didn't like reading before but with all this time to kill it was the perfect escape from the same everyday routine, of course with the occasional shake down from the guards and the seldom shanking of fellow inmates. I acquired a prison nickname, "Papillon" some of you might remember the old Steve McQueen, Dustin Hoffman prison movie, Papillon. I liked that name and wore it proudly, what a coincidence that as much as I liked Steve McQueen movies this guy just began calling me that. I also picked up jogging and I began jogging 3 times a week. I thought I had everything under control but inside of me I was in so much pain. I needed to talk to someone but to whom, who could I trust? Weekdays we had work and chores and on weekends there was too much time to think and I didn't like that. I wanted to keep busy and have the time fly by. On Sundays I decided to go to church but Catholic services was just one hour so I went to all Christian services. There was one group that I began attending where there was a Pastor that was not an inmate who would come to talk to us. He had also been an inmate in a prison and told us his incredible story. How he had found God in prison and how Jesus Christ had saved him from death. He served his time and became a Pastor, married, and had kids. Ok I was interested and I wanted to know what else he had to say. Now, I know that in prison it's said that people either find death or find God and that it's all a cliché but those are sayings from those who've never been in prison that have no idea of the fear inside these walls. I grasped onto the idea that I wanted to know God and not death. Every Sunday I walked my sad butt into that room and listened to inmate's stories and some were fascinating. I was beginning to feel the stress lessen slightly; I had a feeling of purpose and it was to learn what was being taught to me in prison. I was feeling a little safer and protected, but one night I dreamt that I was getting raped and I was trying to get away but the person was too strong. This person was laughing at me and I looked back to see who it was and it was the Devil! I yelled for help but couldn't get away and he just laughed at me! I woke up scared and I prayed for help, and thanked that it was a nightmare. That dream brought me down and I started feeling that fear again of insecurity. I tried to keep busy with my chores and going to church. I was also trying to stay out of trouble and keep away from those that looked for trouble. But there was a certain Cuban guy that decided to cause trouble for me, because I was quiet. "Hey Gilberto, so what makes you so important that you come here and not have to pay your do's?! I had to pay my do's why shouldn't you? Well you better start paying your do's to me and you better do what I say!" I didn't speak to him and he walked away. I was so angry and I wanted to retaliate but he was Cuban and was protected. I couldn't touch him without permission and knowing this place he was also probably armed with a shank. I went to speak with the Cuban leader and explained what was going on. He gave me bad news, "Gilberto he is one of us, we can't protect you from him, and you'd better do what he says." Now I was hopeless and I didn't know what to do. Daily this guy began coming around and giving me orders, but I was too old to take orders from some jackass. I'd simply ignore him and piss him off but he got the message I was sending. He came at me angry one day and tried to hit me but I was not going to let him. We started fighting and began exchanging blows. I was expecting for a shank to come out and for me to die, but it never did and I didn't die. The guards came and separated us and gave us their beat down. He looked at me and told me in Spanish "You're a dead man Gilberto!" They searched both of us and I noticed that he did not have any weapon on him. I felt I had been given another chance to live that day, but we were placed in solitary confinement. That small room with no windows had such a psychological effect on us that it made some men cry, but I saw it as another day to live. I mentioned my situation to the guards but they really couldn't do too much to help me, so I asked for them to leave me in solitary confinement, and they did. The small room was torture; I didn't know what time it was or what day it was. I tried to sleep my time away but you could only sleep so much. With nothing else to do and no one to turn to, I began to cry and pray. "Why? Why?!!! Why me God?! I need your help, I need you to protect me God; please don't let me die in here! I want to live and see my family again, please!!!" Fear set in my soul, my stomach tightened, my body tensed up, and my teeth grinded together. My heart cried out loud with pain, my chest hurt from my muscles contracting so hard, my gasps for air followed by vomiting and the process would repeat; pain in my heart, stomach, exhaling all my strength, then gasp again. I had never felt so scared and alone in my life. All I could do was beg and plea with God to protect me from this man. Day after day I kneeled down crying and calling out to God; these were the most painful days. I could only think about my circumstances, that I had never killed anybody neither directly nor indirectly, and I didn't want to kill this man because it meant I could get charged and have my sentence extended for murder and never leave this place. Even though I was in that small room, the prison rumors would still reach me. The rumor was that he was going to kill me as soon as I got out. Fear had covered me completely and I wanted to hide in that small room and stay inside until my sentence was over. The days were counting down until the guards had to let me out from here. I was running out of hope and began facing the fact that I would die. I had 3 days till I was out when I heard some favorable news. This Cuban guy had more enemies and had angered his Cuban associates that they stopped protecting him. That opened the door for all his enemies to come to collect and they did.

The Colored fellas got to him first and had their way with him then proceeded to beat him down almost till death, but the guards reached him before he was killed. He was sent to the hospital and was in critical condition. I didn't wish death on anyone but this news made me very happy because my persecutor was taken away. I was thankful for what had happened.

Out of solitary confinement I knew I had to get out of this prison somehow. Visiting day came and I saw my wife, and I told Piedad all that had happened. She was so scared and told me that she had been praying for me every day. I told her that I wanted an appeal and she agreed, but we would have to use the last of our savings. Many inmates after being sentenced would request an appeal for their cases to see if their sentence could be lowered. I then started my appeal to see what could happen. My previous lawyer had promised so much good and asked for so much money but finally never delivered. He never gave me any money back nor could I complain to anyone. It was legal theft, he knew that I didn't have a chance but asked for more money anyway. He knew once I was sentenced I couldn't accuse him of anything. Well some say that sometimes payback is better than Christmas! As I requested my appeal I learned that my lawyer had done the same to other inmates asking for large amounts of cash and stealing it once we went to prison. I also learned that this Dirty Rat Sapo lawyer was an informant for the cops and would listen to client's secrets and give all that information to the cops, which they in return would prosecute us with the same information. This guy was a dirt bag, lower than scum, piece of trash! I and all the inmates that had been represented by this Dirty Rat Sapo started a case against him for all the wrong he did. My request for appeal was in, now I had to wait and have faith, but it was going to take a few years just to hear something back from the court.

I also started a request for transfer to a closer prison to Tampa because this place was too far for my family to visit every weekend. I talked to the administration here so they could move me quickly but they were not very helpful. They just figured that I was some inmate that needed to suffer some more while I served my time. I was stressing so much that my ulcers began to irritate me severely and I had to go to the clinic frequently. Blood was appearing in my stool meaning that the ulcers were serious. The Doctor saw me many times and then told me basically that I was bleeding inside. I had been suffering from ulcers since I was a kid in Colombia because of the way I would not eat in school from the lack of money. At this time in medicine there was a cure for ulcers, they discovered that it was some bacteria in the stomach that caused the ulcers. The Doc started me on some antibiotics to treat and eventually cure my ulcers after decades of suffering with this, thank God. Now I had nothing else to do but wait for time to take its course.

Problems in prison were no joke and I found myself in church asking for miracles, for protection, for healing, to win my appeal, and for my freedom. God began teaching me so many things in prison that I thought I knew but I was so blind before. I started questioning the Pastor about all that he knew. I began paying more attention in the service and bought a Bible to study it. The things I was learning were incredible; I had read some of the Bible before but now I understood it better. The Pastor showed me how wrong I was just by reading the 1st Commandment. "We say we believe in God, we say we are Christians, but do we know what God is telling us?" I thought I did. "The 1st Commandment, Exodus 20:3 says; 'You shall have no other gods before me.' In Matthew 22:36-37 Jesus says when asked which is the great commandment of the Law? He answered. 'You shall love the Lord your God with all your heart, with all your soul, and with all your mind.' "Do you worship God?" We all thought the same thing, 'but we go to church.' Then he said, "Worshipping God is showing that you love Him by obeying Him the same way you show you love your parents, obeying them. Matthew 22:38-40 Jesus says, 'the second commandment is like it: You shall love your neighbor as yourself. On these two commandments depends all the Law and the Prophets.' Do you love or hate your neighbor?" Okay I get it I hate everyone, but I was no murderer, no thief, I'm sure God would give me a pass, I hope. I knew then that I had been using God like a genie in a bottle when I needed something I rubbed my lamp, asked for my wish, and then put it away thinking that God served us, then getting mad at God if He didn't give you what you wanted. But I never listened to what He might have to say to me. The Bible says that the blessings come after the obedience, but I had never really been obedient to what the Bible says. I learned that for God sin is sin and sin brings death and there's no difference in sins to Him. I stopped lying to myself and saw that I had violated all the commandments except murder and I did have other gods I bowed down to, I swore, I was a liar, an adulterer, and a thief. I was a criminal, a drug dealer, and I was even an abusive husband, and father. I deserved death as well as everyone on this planet, but that's why Jesus came, the name Jesus means, 'God saves.' God put all of our evil works on Jesus. Hundreds of years before the birth of Jesus, Isaiah 53:3-7 says about Jesus: He was despised and rejected by men; a man of sorrows, and acquainted with grief; and as one from whom men hide their faces he was despised, and we esteemed him not. Surely he has borne our grief and carried our sorrows; yet we esteemed him stricken, smitten by God, and afflicted. But he was wounded for our transgressions; he was crushed for our iniquities; upon him was the chastisement that brought us peace, and with his stripes we are healed. All we like sheep have gone astray; we have turned—everyone—to his own way; and the Lord has laid on him the iniquity of us all." When I heard all of this I was ashamed and asked God for forgiveness. I had been a jerk to my family for so long and I thought I was such a great person.

After months of working, reading, running, and attending all the Christian services on Sundays my ulcer problem was cured, and I heard news from my case. My new lawyer was fighting to have the State drop the charges on the cocaine found in my house since there was no search warrant. That was great news for me because it was the major decision factor in my case. My transfer came through and I was sent to a prison closer to my family but it was a prison where inmates had gone crazy from all the stress. I had to suck it up because at the end this place was a little calmer than normal prison, but its downside was that everyone was crazy. I guess I exaggerated too much to the Doctors about my condition. It was not long before I got familiar with things in here and I met others that were not crazy and in the same situation as I. My cellmate was definitely crazy and frequently would begin yelling "There coming to get me! Help me please!" There were others that just stared into oblivion with drool on their face. And there were those that talked to themselves always as if conversing with someone invisible. I was starting to think that the crazies would make me crazy, oh man. I learned to just keep to myself or meet the others that were not crazy. In here everyone had to see the Doctor often and I miraculously began showing signs of improvement. I made it clear to the Doc that my stress was produced from being so far from my family. I was there for almost a year but soon got transferred again. The Doctor made a request to have me transferred to a prison in Zephyrhills, which was very close to Tampa and that was perfect for my family. I got off the bus at Zephyrhills, took a few months to get familiarized with things, and avoided things that could get you killed. Piedad was happy about my transfer and now I would receive visits on Wednesdays and Saturdays, it was great. In this prison I met all kinds of people and we had nothing else to do than to tell each other our stories. I heard amazing stories like one of a cat burglar that stole priceless jewels from famous Jewelry stores sneaking his way through the ventilation ducts and never getting caught; also stealing from rich people when they were on vacation. Other stories of men that had also sold drugs and had made fortunes that would still be there when they got out. I made some friends here and one had a particular sad story he told.

PAUL A. LOPEZ

He had been a famous clown on a TV show and had lots of money. His wife and he had a daughter together but they started having trouble and his wife accused him of sexually abusing their daughter. Their daughter was too young to defend her father and he was convicted. She took all his money and never let him see his daughter again. My story was ok I guess but some seemed to like it too.

My years in prison were going by slowly and I continued to attend services on Sundays. This Sunday was unique though. I had attended for years now and the Pastor preached similar stories and asked for those that wanted to ask for forgiveness and to except the Lord, but this time he wanted to lay hands on us. This means that he goes around the room putting his hand on our foreheads and praying for us to receive the Holy Spirit. In many previous services I had seen people get touched and then fall down, but I thought it was ridiculous, needless to say I was highly skeptical. He went around the room and when he came to me, I braced myself so I would not fall. I doubted that this was possible and that the pastor might just push me down. But when he stepped in front of me he said, "Receive the Spirit of God." The next thing I know, I am on the floor, and he had already moved from me quite a distance, meaning that I was unconscious. What happened? Did he hit me that hard? But what I felt was an indescribable feeling of peace in my heart; I felt an awesome presence that warmed my entire body. Tears ran down my face and I knew that this day God had touched me. I felt like a new man wanting never to return to that ogre I had been for years. I made a promise to God saying that if he got me out from this place that I would be a good man.

I had been in prison now for almost 2 years and since then I'd missed so many great family moments. Luckily I had made it to my older sons High School Graduation before I was locked up, but since that he had married his girlfriend and she was pregnant. I was going to be a Grandfather but unable to attend any birthdays or build great memories. My younger son was now in High School and soon he would graduate, wow how time flies! My poor wife had been working 3 jobs to pay the bills and would take our younger son to help her. I was more of a burden to them than a help since instead of sending them money they had to send me money. I was using all that I had saved on my appeal and the lawyer representing me. My lawyer visited on occasion to update me on my case, but this day was special. "Gilberto so far in your case we know that the drugs that were retrieved from your vehicle was lost due to contamination of the evidence, and I'm fighting about the drugs found in your home in a gym bag without a proper Search Warrant. I also have good news about your former lawyer that supposedly was working as an informant for the State. He had so many complaints and lawsuits against him that he lost his BAR license, meaning that he cannot practice criminal law anymore!" Wow, I was speechless! It's incredible having the judicial system also work for your benefit. "Thank you for all your help," was all I could say to him. Piedad and I were happy for a change and I was feeling freedom very close. I was also getting word from my friends about those still in the business and all the things that had changed in these last 2 years. I heard that the guy that tried to kill El Negro and I had been arrested, served time in Texas, and in Florida for attempted murder then he was deported to Colombia. In Colombia he didn't last too long, El Negro's family caught up with him and made him disappear for good. I also heard that El Negro walked with a limp now and that he had sent word to me saying that he was very grateful to me for saving his life that night that I also got shot. It was nice knowing that I did save his life that night and that we both survived that ordeal.

Almost three years in prison and I got to meet my grandson Anthony. He was so cute and looked a lot like my two sons when they were babies. Paul was a happy father and I wanted to tell him to be a better dad than I was and that I was sorry for being the jerk I was. On visiting days when I got to see them I began telling my sons and my wife all the things I was learning in Church and the new man I was through Jesus Christ. They seemed to pay very close attention to me and I hoped it was not too late to redeem myself a little from the Ogre I was before. I had learned so many things about myself and I recognized that I was filled with hate and still so very angry and hurt from when I was a child and how everyone in my family including my mother rejected me. I was looking for their approval all the time and thought if I was a rich man that they would love me. My Pastor had also told me one thing that I will remember forever. He said, "Gilberto many men have this problem but don't know they have it until it's too late, and that's farsightedness." "What?" "You are farsighted, your vision only sees what's far from you and everything near you is blurry, boring, and out of focus." I really didn't understand at first because I had very good vision. But he continued, "Not your physical eyes man, but your spiritual ones, let me explain. You have always had what you needed very close: your wife, your kids, and your freedom, which in turn should bring you happiness. But your farsightedness makes all things near you dull, blurry, and you can't focus on what's really important. You can only see what's far from you: better looking women, better cars, better house, and better clothes. But as soon as you get closer to some of those things they are dull, blurry, and boring again; that's farsightedness. But God wants you to be nearsighted so you can see all the special gifts he has given you." I understood what he meant and he was right. I had thrown my freedom away searching things I didn't really need because I thought they would make me happy. When all that really made me happy was being with my family and I had been so close to throwing it all away. I wanted another chance to make it right but I needed to behave and get out soon. But when things are going well is when all hell breaks loose. We were all in our rooms when the Corrections Officers came yelling and having us all go outside. We were all trying to find out what was going on as we were herded out to the fields. "What's happening?" The rumors began to hum in the crowd. "Someone was killed earlier today, and the Officers are doing their "Shake Down" looking for any weapons or drugs." "Who was killed, does anybody know?" Everyone was asking the same questions and eventually the answer would come to us in minutes by word of mouth. "Yea it was those two love birds, Jackson and Ramirez. Apparently it was a lover's quarrel and it seems that Ramirez did Jackson wrong so Jackson killed him." We were outside for almost 2 hours and we found out that Ramirez and Jackson were in a relationship and arguing. Jackson went into a jealous rage and began beating Ramirez but then pulled out the nearest sprinkler head from the grass and beat poor Ramirez's head in leaving a bloody mess. This was the horrible carnage we were exposed to on a normal basis. Just as I was thinking that all was ok the Officers called me into a room and had me stripped searched which you can imagine is very humiliating for a man in his 40's. "Lopez we found drugs in your shoes!" I was shocked and replied, "That's impossible I don't use drugs." "We found some pill in your shoe and it's off to the lab to get analyzed, but you know until it gets back you're going into the hole!" I was mad because I knew it wasn't mine and now I was going to be put in solitary confinement until they knew what is was. Then I remembered that I had bought those shoes from a cellmate and I told the guards, but of course they figured I was lying. Last time I was in solitary confinement I was very scared, but this time I grabbed onto the word of God and his promises. I took my bible with me and just read while I waited until I was let go. It was a constant battle in my brain, it playing with me telling me that I was going to be held longer for having drugs on me, but I had to remember the word of God. Psalm 23, The Lord is my Sheppard. A few days later the Officers came and let me go, then said I was ok, the lab results showed it was just some antacid or something. "Hallelujah!!!" I knew now that I had to read the Bible, pray, and have faith in the word of God, so I did just that.

After 2 years and nine months I received a letter in the mail from the courts. I knew exactly what it was and I was very afraid to open it. I took it to my Pastor and he also knew what it was. "Do you want me to open it Gilberto?" "Yes please, I can't do it myself because I am too afraid to see what it says." I was in the prison chapel with only the Pastor and some friends. He opened the envelope and began reading it to himself while I watched the look on his face. He said that the end was confusing and that I needed to read it. My heart was beating so hard that I felt every beat in my head; I took the letter and began reading it. There was so much legal lingo but at the end it sort of read like this, "Mr. Lopez after carefully reviewing your case repeatedly and considering all the extenuating circumstances involved in such case we have decided to drop your charges." I felt my spirit jump with incredible joy and happiness! I could not believe what I had read and read it again and again. My Pastor, friends, and I praised God for this huge miracle. When I had requested my appeal, everyone told me that it was impossible to win and that I would be here till 2010. I refused to believe them and filed for appeal anyway, but they would always say that everyone who filed for an appeal always lost. There is nothing impossible for God and deep inside me I had that hope and faith that I would win. When the other inmates heard, the good hearted ones were happy for me but many others were angry at me with envy. My lawyer called me and told me when I would be freed and he told my wife the good news. The next couple of days all I did was praise God and Thank Him for this huge miracle. It was the summer of 1998 when I was freed and all my family and my two true friends were there to celebrate with me. It was a spectacular feeling and the party celebrating my freedom was awesome!!! I had learned that God doesn't speak to us with audible words but with His written words from the Bible, He also spoke to us with actions and you all must know by now that Actions speak louder than Words! Everything I had asked God for that I needed I had received, and after all the pain I had gone through I had learned so much about Him in my life, and this is why I believe in Him. I wanted to tell everyone about God and the miracles He did for me in my most desperate time of need.

Chapter Eight

A SECOND CHANCE

Ok Dad it's your son Paul again calling to ask you more about your life. Are you ready? Hi son I'm ready, where were we by the way? Yeah you were telling me how God had performed another great miracle in your life by getting you out early. Oh yeah that's right, He did and this is what happened afterward . . .

. . . .

I had been locked up for 2 years and 10 months in prison. Free again, very grateful, and so much had changed. I can't imagine if I would've been in prison till 2010, how would things be then? Again finding a job was easy because I knew so many people in the restaurant business. I knew that this was my life, and that I had to find contentment in what I knew until I knew how to do something else. My wife was able to quit her part time jobs, and my youngest son could now focus on school again and not worry about having to help his mother with the part time jobs. My oldest son had been busy since I left. He had gotten his girlfriend pregnant and had married her, but when I was out from prison he was getting divorced from her. Their relationship had not been a good one and unfortunately he had lots of anger issues, most likely from what he learned from me. I saw him very down and broken up from his divorce and because he couldn't be with his son every day. Piedad and I felt so bad for him and he soon moved back in with us. My brother Juan who had been living in Colombia and had so much money and property had lost everything and had come back to the States and was living in Atlanta. It was such a shame and incredible how both him and I had lost everything that we bought with the business money. As the months went by I was running into old associates and they were all glad that I was out already and they were all eager to know how? Unfortunately when I would tell them that I came to know God through Jesus Christ in prison and that God gave me a miracle, not all who listened were interested and did not believe. Some would say "Wow you're so lucky!" and others would say, "Well good for you man." I told my story to my few friends and family and they were amazed on how God kept me safe in the middle of that hell. With this second chance I wanted to be the ideal husband and father since I had been such an ogre for so long. My oldest son did not handle his divorce well and rashly joined the US Marines to get away. He would leave to boot camp later in the fall. My brother Juan came down from Atlanta and began living with us until he could live on his own again. It seemed like history was repeating itself from when we came here in the 80's. But this time we were not interested in selling drugs again! I had learned my lesson and so had my brother Juan, we didn't want anything to do with drugs anymore. We had lived ambitious lives but it was all smoke and mirrors, a big lie, and all it brought us was trouble. We were back to living honest lives with real jobs. We began having parties and going to the beaches in big groups but with a more modest attitude this time. Everything was back to the way it was before the drug business and I actually did feel happy. Yeah sometimes I did miss the money, but I didn't have to look over my shoulder anymore or think that I could get arrested for something illegal or think about the other horrible things that were involved in selling drugs. I felt free, no more guilt, and most importantly I was happy with my family again.

I never had imagined all the terrible consequences that came with selling drugs because I was not out of the woods yet like I thought I was. Two years from when I was freed immigration began calling me and they eventually paid me a visit. They quickly broke the bad news to me, "Mr. Lopez since you are a Resident and not a Legal Citizen yet, and you were arrested and convicted of a felony we must inform you that in the process of becoming a Citizen you must not be charged with any felonies, but since you were, you cannot become a Citizen hence forfeiting your Residency of the United States and facing DEPORTATION." Oh God, another obstacle to face, I was heartbroken and my family and I didn't know how to react to the news. Immigration told me that I had a few months to appeal but then I would be deported to Colombia. That put a damper in my happiness and all I could do now was appeal. Finding an honest lawyer is very difficult to do but I found 2 and they both told me the truth and not what I wanted to hear. My case was not worth fighting and spending money on anymore lawyers. The law was written saying that you cannot be found guilty for any felonies or plead No contest, meaning that I would eventually be deported. With no other solutions I had to accept the fact that I would be kicked out of the USA! I prayed and I pleaded with God to keep me with my family, not to let me be deported, and to rescue me from this fate.

A year later immigration was knocking at my door again. I opened the door, "Sir are you Gilberto Lopez?" and as soon as I said yes, they arrested, cuffed, and took me away again. This time I was taken and held in an immigration jail until they had enough Colombians to deport together. I guess the airlines gave the government discount airfare for a bundle of deported immigrants or something. Ha ha ha . . . You have to keep your sense of humor in the midst of this cruel world. What I found ridiculous was that it was taking a few months to collect enough people for us to catch our plane; I was getting impatient in jail and wanted to leave already. But soon enough we had a good number of deportees and they took us to the airport where they filled a 737 with all of us. Can you imagine if they would've sent all of us on a civilian flight? How scared all the passengers would've been. Anyway 3 hours later and we had arrived in Bogota, Colombia. The Customs Officers saw us and stamped our passports and we were labeled deportees from the United States of America. I was part of a despicable group, those that were given the chance to come to America, the land of the free and home of the brave, the country where dreams were born, America the beautiful, the land that God had blessed and had made the most powerful country in the whole world. I had the greatest opportunity that any man or woman could have ever been given and I threw it away because of my jealous envy and the desire of being rich. All I could do was hate myself for my stupid blindness, for all the pain and anguish I had caused my family.

Now I was back in the city where I was born, where all my dreams had begun and sadly where all my dreams had died, how ironic. All I did was cry and wonder how different things would have been if I had not done what I did. How happy my wife and children would be with their family together and their father keeping them safe from pain and sadness. If I would've showed my wife, the woman I loved, the woman who stood by me through thick and thin, through sickness and health, through richer or poorer, that I loved her so much and that I missed every second of my life. Why was I not nice when I could've been? Why didn't I show my kids that I loved them and hugged them more? Why did I cause them so much pain? I regretted the way I had been to them and now how could I make things better if I was hundreds of miles away from them? I was so deeply depressed that I did not want to eat, I did not want to talk, and I did not want to live anymore.

"Gilberto wake up! Get up cousin, you cannot sit around here and just throw your life away! You have to see the positive side of things here. You are alive and you haven't lost your family yet, they still love you and they still look for you!

You still have some property here in Colombia and in the States so wake up, shake it off, and get back on that horse man! Things are not over yet, you're not finished yet, and you're not dead yet!" Who is this person saying all these crazy motivational words? I looked around the room and saw one of my brothers, but it wasn't him then I saw a dirty, bearded, old bald man in the room. "Who are you?" "I'm your cousin Antonio." When I saw him I was shocked, mad, but also curious of why he was there and why he was so filthy. Just a reminder, it was Antonio who talked to me in Miami about the business in the 80's and it was his drugs I was arrested for in 95', but I knew very well that it had been my choice to sell drugs and I could not blame anybody but myself for my own choices; I'd learned that in prison. "Antonio what are you doing here Primo?" And he began to tell me his story: "Gilberto remember me when I was rich in the 80's? I drank too much and I was a horrible person and treated my wife badly by beating her when I was drunk. I was arrested for selling cocaine in the 80's, I served my time, but my wife divorced me taking any money I thought I had. My son did not want anything to do with me either because of the abuse I gave his mother and I eventually lost contact with her and my son which hurts me immensely. Again I was arrested for the same thing and served a short sentence, but as soon as I got out immigration came for me." He had been in Colombia a year already but unlike me, he had nothing and was actually homeless, and that's why he was so filthy. He was living in the streets as a beggar and lived off the charity of strangers. My brother Joel saw him in the street begging one day, recognized him, and tried to help him. His story was very sad and my heart felt sad for him and we had him clean up, but unfortunately Antonio had gone through so much anguish and stress that he was not all there, he had gone a little crazy and sometimes would forget things and get aggressive. Helping him was not going to be easy, but his condition showed me that mine was not as bad as others and it helped me wake up from that dangerous depression I was in. I spoke with Piedad on occasion, and I was not in some prison so it wasn't too bad. I did have an apartment in Colombia which was rented out and brought me some cash which was also good, and Piedad had the house in Tampa too. Looking at my whole picture, my situation was not that terrible, but I wanted to be with my wife and kids and I didn't want to settle for anything else.

There were countless stories of Colombians that had walked across the border all the time. I heard of certain friends that had been deported and returned through the border and were safe with their families again. I was a stubborn mule and wanted to be with my family safe again so I began to plan my return to the

States and by now it was cheaper and easier to get across since people had been doing it for years. I took the money out of the bank and made arrangements to sneak through the border, "El Hueco" here I come for the third time again. "We're boarding passengers now for Panama." That was my call to get on the plane and I waved bye to my family. First Panama, next Mexico, then the United States; it all seemed simple now to me after all I had been through. I arrived in Mexico where I once again met with Coyotes to get me across the Rio Grande. There were several others with me following the Coyote, some for the first time that had that worried look on their faces, and others like me that had crossed the borders more than once showing more confidence, but some of these people were experts at crossing because of their numerous times back and forth, it was incredible how these people worked in the States, saved their money, would go to their country to visit family, and then return to work in the States again crossing through the border constantly. What a sense of persistency, tenacity, courage, motivation, and dedication these people demonstrated to keep their families fed and clothed back home. Unfortunately they are not viewed in that manner, but that of being a nuisance to the Country and its economy. And to a degree I understood how illegal immigrants caused an imbalance in the economy, but I also knew that the only thing we cared about was the welfare of our families. Meaning that if there aren't enough well-paid jobs to keep us in our own countries then we, the people are going to find a way and find jobs where ever that might be. We weren't just going to sit around and die of starvation. So here we were around 10 of us trying to sneak through the Mexican/American border to either be with our families or find work to support our families, which is more than enough motivation to risk your freedom, health, and life.

Spring of 2001 near the Mexican border in a remote area of Texas stood a maximum state penitentiary and on a particularly dark night several dangerous inmates made a break for it and were able to escape from this prison. The inmates had scattered themselves to avoid capture but the most obvious route was the Mexican border. The US Marshalls, Texas Rangers, along with law enforcement officers from the entire State of Texas were looking for these fugitives and they had created roadblocks all around the state but were highly concentrated on the border. The strategy was proven to work as they nabbed some fugitives trying to leave, but it proved to work so well that it was catching others trying to come into the States also. Just picture this, a big group of happy illegal immigrants crossing the border into the States thinking about their families and how great things were going to be but unknowingly walking right into the spiders web and being greeted by numerous uniformed officers, suited up officials, all of them wearing their bullet proof vests with FBI and Marshalls written on them, and these uniformed men having their trusty M16 rifles pointed at all of us as one man on a megaphone was yelling in Spanish and English, "Manos Arriba!!! Hands up!!!" "**Hay Chihuahua!!!**" came from someone in our group and in a blink of an eye I saw those happy faces turn into frowns including mine. The first timers cried, the more than once group were sad, but the experts were neither scared, nor sad because they knew they'd be coming back soon. All I could think was, "Why Me!!!!" We were taken to the city jail then transferred to an immigration jail where I let Piedad know where I was. She was furious with me because everyone tried to tell me to stay in Colombia, but I didn't listen to them or to my inner voice saying not to do it. I saw the judge and he gave me my sentence. "Mr. Lopez for you and others like you that have been deported already you were told that if caught inside the States again it would be an automatic 3 years in prison." Thinking back, I do remember them saying that to me. Wow was I a fool or what? I was jailed for selling drugs, won my appeal and was out early, deported, then jailed again because I came back illegally. You couldn't make this stuff up! This was truly embarrassing and I was ashamed of myself. Now I was going to have to endure another 3 years behind bars.

Eden, Texas 2001; I was an inmate again in some Immigration Jail. When I heard the name of the town I imagined something like the Garden of Eden, a paradise on Earth, but as soon as I got my glimpse of the landscape outside of the fence I sadly realized someone had been sarcastic when naming this place. As far as I could see were plains of dry grass and some trees but nothing else. All I could do to ease my frustration was to do what I did the first time in jail, keep myself busy. Again I began going to the library and reading books, going to church, and I started running every day. I read the book "Papillon" which was way better than the movie. I read other numerous great books one after the other that I needed reading glasses. I continued to skim through the Bible and **coincidently** found a verse that said 'If you make a promise to the Lord, make sure to keep it or else He will hold you accountable.' I quickly remembered that I constantly made promises to God and would ask him for a favor but when God came through I quickly forgot my promise. When I was in prison the first time I prayed to God to get me out and I promised to never break the law again. God came through for me and I was out 12 years earlier but then forgot my promise and I broke the law again by coming in the States illegally. Wow so many things in this book called the Bible that was incredible still to this day. It was so mysterious and confusing but I was learning that the more I studied it, the more it was making sense. Was God trying to tell me something, was He trying to teach me how to live right, was the God of the Jews and the Gentiles trying to talk to me? I was starting to feel that He wanted to take care of me and guide me the right way.

Every morning we were woken up, taken to breakfast, made to work, and then given free time in the late afternoons. I made my schedule around theirs; and I would go running, showered, and then I would read. On Sundays I was in church learning the Bible again. Today I read Matthew 6:19-21, and I'm paraphrasing, that "Not to create for ourselves treasures on earth where moth, rust, and thieves destroy, but to create for ourselves treasures in Heaven where they cannot destroy. For where your treasure is there your heart will be also." Also in verse 24 it said that "No one can serve two masters, for either he will hate the one and love the other. You cannot serve God and money." It was making sense to me because my only focus in life was making money to buy things and when I made it big all I served was my money and never God, and in my heart all I wanted was more money. At the end everything I had made was taken from me faster than I made it. But according to the Bible it said to trust in God and He will give you everything you need. Matthew 6:25-33 spoke about trusting fully in God. "Therefore I tell you, do not be anxious about your life, what you will eat or what you will drink, nor about your body, what you will put on. Is not life more than food and the body more than clothing? Look at the birds of the air: they neither sow nor reap nor gather into barns, and yet your heavenly Father feeds them. Are you not of more value than they? And which of you by being anxious can add a single hour to his span of life? And why are you anxious about clothing? Consider the lilies of the field how they grow: they neither toil nor spin, yet I tell you, even Solomon in all his glory was not arrayed like one of these. But if God so clothes the grass of the field, which today is alive and tomorrow is thrown into the oven, will He not much clothe you, O you of little faith? Therefore do not be anxious, saying 'What shall we eat?' or 'What shall we drink?' or 'What shall we wear?' For the Gentiles seek after all these things, and your heavenly Father knows that you need them all. But seek first the kingdom of God and his righteousness, and all these things will be added to you." As I read these words I was amazed but also challenged. How was I going to trust in these words? But then I remembered all the times that God did come through for me and I knew that I had to try. I really wanted to have that faith in God and trust in Him to guide me through my decisions and place Him at the wheel of my life.

Visiting days came and went but Piedad could only visit me occasionally since I was in Texas and not in Florida. She came to visit me this time and told me what she had to do to get here. "Gordo, I took a few days off from work, flew into San Antonio, rented a car at the airport, and still had to drive 4 hours to get here." This place was so far from home that it was very expensive just to come and visit for a few hours a day. My family and the few friends I had could not afford to make the trip so for the years to come I had to be fine with letters or phone calls. I had to really dive into my schedule and keep busy. As the months crept by I lost so much wait from jogging that my wife couldn't call me "Gordo" anymore, Gordo was my nickname she had for me meaning Fat. I was in better shape now than before. Even though so far away from my family news from my past came to me. I spoke to my Brother Juan who told me that most of our friends that kept in the drug business were also losing everything because the Law had made business really hard and they were catching people faster with better technology. The amount of drugs being smuggled was drastically cut in half and hurting most of their profit. Juan also told me about our old supplier in Colombia that had decided to smuggle weapons instead of drugs and figured out that smuggling weapons is the worst thing anybody can do according to the Law. He had been shipping drugs across the border for years and was never caught but as soon as he began trying to ship weapons Interpol got involved and soon after he was arrested and facing life in prison. I could not believe my ears especially because that person was already rich but still wanted more money. People in this world were silly and I realized that the Rich just get Greedier while the Poor just get Needier. All I knew was that no matter if Rich or Poor we should learn to treat each other with kindness and respect. This is the Golden Rule: Matthew 6:12; "So whatever you wish that others would do to you, do also to them, for this is the Law and the Prophets." I still had a lot to learn regarding my spiritual communication with God but I know that we are a working progress and God gave me a second chance to be a better person with Jesus as my Lord and Savior.

January of 2004 rolled around and I had served my sentence. My dedication to my schedule and keeping busy studying the Bible made these years feel like days. And I was freed after almost three years in a Texas prison. Soon I was boarding a plane with other Colombians again. We all joked around in the plane, and one said "Wave goodbye to the USA and the gringos." So I did, I said Goodbye to the

PAUL A. LOPEZ

United States. As for me I knew that I would never try coming back here unless I was invited. America had given me the best years of my life and Lady Liberty did open her arms to my family. I had been able to care for my family and bring them with me. My dreams were coming true slowly but surely but greed destroyed that for me. For my family their dreams were beginning to come true. They were all US Citizens and were living good lives. My wife kept working in whatever possible and God took care of her. She had worked three jobs and paid all the debt I left behind. She was also able to keep the house that we lived in and our family helped her out. My oldest son was a United States Marine serving the country that gave him freedom. My youngest son was in school studying for his future, a future that was paid for by this country. "Goodbye United States of America, AKA: La USA, AKA: Nueva York." I apologized to her, "I'm sorry for the years that I broke your laws, I'm sorry for the lives I possibly ruined, I'm sorry for the trouble and money I cost you. I apologize to the American people for not being the model Citizen that you asked for when inviting immigrants into your land. I apologize for abusing your generosity, and your patience." I also thanked her for the many good years I had in the States, for the wonderful American friends I had made, and all the people I'd met from all around the world. I was going to miss her tall skyscrapers, and giant highways, the wonderful memories I had living here; the great Hollywood movies I grew up with and the amazing Rock and Roll music I danced to. I was going to miss her great abundance of everything you could think of. Thank You America for those happy years of my life. Thank You America for my family's dreams coming true. And Thank You America for introducing me to the One True God, Jehovah, and our Savior Jesus Christ. Always remain faithful to Him and never leave His commandments and May His Holy Spirit walk with you for many more centuries. Thank You . . .

. . . THE END . . .

CONCLUSION

As a young husband and father with so much disadvantage and so much responsibility my father unfortunately made some horrible mistakes in life causing all of us lots of pain. And yes I did resent him very much at first for all the pain and heartache he put us through. I knew that I did not want to be like my father because of the way he was, but the years in writing this book and interviewing him I actually learned more about him. I discovered that I'm very much like him. I have his bad temper and rash outbursts, but like him I also have his passion and huge heart. I learned why he was that way and why I was also that way. We both needed to know how to love and how to forgive and I forgave my father. My mother had never stopped praying for all of us and thankfully a faithful woman's prayers were heard and God intervened. Through my father's poor decisions and hard consequences of life we all learned great lessons. We truly learned that the love of money is the root of all evil. We also recognized that our family had heard of God before but now we know who He is in our lives, and we love Him for what He did for us. Lastly we knew that the only way we would've heard His voice was by feeling the pain caused by our own evil desires then witnessing His everlasting mercy and love. He forgave us, so we chose to serve Him, and He has blessed us ever since transforming our lives forever.

Colombia is my place of birth, she is my first home, and I love Colombia very much. I want to express my love for the Colombian people and my other Latin American brothers and sisters. I want to tell you never to give up. Follow your heart; be true to God, and to yourself. Know that your blood, sweat, and tears in your hard work are not in vain. Keep your love for your family, the true good thing in life. In addition I want to note that thankfully for decades Colombia's government has been working very hard to stabilize the country and build a safer place to live and visit. Since the year 2000 its economy has begun to flourish and since then become very popular worldwide. Colombia has also been transformed into a tourist paradise where people from all around the globe are flocking to see the country's magnificent beauty and meet her passionate people. So I invite you to visit Colombia and you'll see that she is a beautiful place with wonderful

PAUL A. LOPEZ

people. I also want to show my gratitude to my second home, my second place of birth, the United States. Thank you for the opportunities of a lifetime and for giving my family a place to live.

It's 2012 now and since my father's deportation back to Colombia in 2004 we have been living good and happy lives. My mother resides here in the States where she works but also takes long vacations to live with my father in Colombia, and my brother and I visit him when we can and talk to him frequently. Our American Dreams are coming true as we work hard to better ourselves and keeping faithful to our Lord. As for me I served 5 years Active Duty in the United States Marine Corps, came home and worked in Law Enforcement while serving in the Army Reserves for another 3 years. Then I had the urge to tell our story so I did the research and interviewed my father from 2006 to 2008 where I then began writing the book and finished it in 2012. I hope the readers liked our story and I pray that you've learned something from this experience. Thank you and God bless you all.

REFERENCE

"Scripture quotations are from The Holy Bible, English Standard Version (ESV), copyright 2001 by Crossway, a publishing ministry of Good News Publishers. Used by permission. All rights reserved."